Upon My Word!

by the same authors

YOU CAN'T HAVE YOUR KAYAK AND HEAT IT
stories from 'My Word!'

FRANK MUIR & DENIS NORDEN

upon my word!

More stories from 'My Word!'

a panel game devised by
Edward J Mason & Tony Shryane

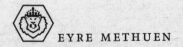

EYRE METHUEN

But still a pun I do detest,
'Tis such a paltry, humbug jest;
They who've least wit can make them best.

William Combe
Dr Syntax in search of the Picturesque

People that make puns are like wanton boys
that put coppers on the railroad tracks.

Oliver Wendell Holmes
The Autocrat of the Breakfast-Table

First published in 1974
by Eyre Methuen Ltd
11 New Fetter Lane, London EC4P 4EE
© 1974 by Frank Muir and Denis Norden
Printed in Great Britain
by T. & A. Constable Ltd
Hopetoun Street, Edinburgh

ISBN 0 413 32660 8

Contents

'The Light That Failed'

Rudyard Kipling
Title of Story

I T'S fair to say that, even at my most unbuttoned, I am
to the Fun People what Marcel Marceau is to radio. For that reason, it
was perhaps unwise even to have considered accepting that invitation
to Bernice's Housecooling Party. Bernice, by common agreement of
every After Eight consumer in the Garden Suburb, is more or less a
registered Fun Person. So for me to receive an invite to one of her
celebrations was very akin to breaking through the Roundhead
lines.

For the benefit of those of you who don't live at that pace either, I
should explain that a Housecooling party is one thrown to mark the
departure from a house. In Bernice's case, this was occasioned by the fact
that she and Lionel had finally split up. I say 'finally' because although
divorce had been on the cards for ages, they'd been trying to make a go
of it for the sake of the home movies.

Now, however, the split was official and Bernice was launching her
new status with champagne and the chums round and I felt no end
chuffed at being included among those cavorting. The only snag was,
what should I take along as a present? What sort of gift is *appropriate*
to a Fun Person? Yes, obviously a Fun *Thing* – but then again, what's
that? I did a tentative wander round our local Gift Boutique, but that's
not really an Aladdin's Cave even at the best of times and especially
not since it branched out into Suede Cleaning and Sheepskin Renewal.

Contact sunglasses? An electric kettle with a stereo whistle? A
musical toilet-roll holder that plays 'Dream The Impossible Dream'?
Everything I considered seemed far too *stolid* for a fun-gift. Then, the
following Sunday, my eye lighted on an item in the newspaper: a
trendy foundry in the Midlands was offering reproduction

chastity-belts! Perfect replicas, in cast iron, of the famed mediaeval securi-corps. complete with padlock and key.

When I presented one to Bernice, I must say its reception proved all I could have hoped for. "Oh, what a Fun Thing!" she ejaculated. "Do look everybody, oh do look!" She's a large lady, Bernice, and as she never wears undergarments, when she walks everything seems to move more than her feet do. Right now, her motion was that of a blancmange in a railway dining-car. "Isn't it a hoot!" she shouted. "Oh, Giorgio, do come and look."

Giorgio turned out to be an Italian water-skiing instructor she'd recently imported from Portofino. About seven-foot tall, sun-tanned, muscles even unto the eyebrows, and didn't speak one word of English. "Isn't it absolutely darling?," she yelled, waving the belt in front of him, "Chastitia Belta!" He nodded uncomprehendingly and grinned, exposing teeth you could read small print by.

"Bags you try it on," shouted the man who manages the Driving School, an ex-major with gin leaking out of his ears. "Go on, Bernice, put it on!"

"Oh I must, I must! Give me just five mins."

While she was upstairs, I was man of the moment. Everybody crowded round me and said what a brilliant idea, what really fun-thinking, how absolutely knockout, and you really must come round to our pad for fondue. And when Bernice came down again, "It fits as if it was made for me," she squealed. "Absolutely superb, darling."

Then, while everybody was uttering cheers and upping their glasses to me, she waved her hands in the air. "A moment's quiet now," she said. "Best of order, please. It's time for Bernice to make the big announcement."

She moved over to Giorgio and leaned back against the brown wall of his chest. "This morning at eleven o'clock, Giorgio and I were married in Hampstead Registry Office. Tonight we're off to Portofino for the honeymoon bit."

A moment's gaping – then whoops and yoicks. Hugging, back-slapping, cries of congratulations from all the males, envy from the females. They poured champagne the way Wimpeys pour concrete and, after someone had put the Marriage Theme from *The Godfather* on the record-player, dancing took place.

So when, an hour or so later, Bernice came quivering up at my side, I was feeling no angst at all. "Just off to change into the going-away gear, darling," she smiled. "Can I have the padlock key?"

"By jove, yes," I chuckled. "Jolly well better have that, I should think, what?" I don't know why I seem to fall into that playing-against-type sort of dialogue in Fun People environments, nerves I suppose, but anyway I reached jovially into my pocket for the small cast-iron key.

It was the first time I ever really comprehended the meaning of that expression "suddenly taken sober". As I groped from pocket to pocket, I could *feel* the room cooling. Slowly all conversation died, the record-player was switched-off, more and more eyes turned to me as I patted myself, poked, dug, scrabbled, tore. By the time I had every single one of my pocket-linings hanging out, the place was in complete silence. The only sound to be heard came from the TV set next door. It was a commercial; the one about "all that locked-in goodness".

"Surely," said somebody finally, "surely they come with a *spare* key."

"Well, no. Not if you think about it," I said. "I mean not for a chastity-belt. A spare key, I mean, it'd sort of defeat the whole . . ." It was a trailing-off kind of statement, because nobody seemed all that interested in pursuing its logic. From upstairs we heard Giorgio burst into sudden song. Having gone up to change into his other tee-shirt, he was cheerfully belting out the Italian version of "Tonight, tonight, Won't be just any night."

"Send for the Fire Brigade," said Bernice, her eyes never leaving mine and all that mighty mass at rest.

The first thing the Head Fireman said when he came through the door was "Will I need the extension ladder?" I took him out on to the patio and gave him a complete, if muttered, explanation of the circumstances. He stared at me. "I've got two engines and an appliance out there," he said. "We've halted the traffic up as far as Swiss Cottage."

"An appliance," I said. "That's exactly what's needed. Some kind of appliance."

He shouldered the hose and spoke a few dismissive words into a walkie-talkie. As the mighty engines roared into life and started moving away, he said, "Don't you know it's an offence to make unnecessary 999 calls? I'll lend you a six-inch cold file and consider yourself lucky."

Clutching the ugly metal implement he'd pushed into my hand, I said to Bernice, "Let's go up in the bathroom then." When I felt the little stir of air caused by a whole roomful of eyebrows lifting, I quickly added, "I'll wear some kind of blindfold, of course. Whole thing won't take more than a few minutes."

Nor would it have done. Except that Giorgio, sensing his new

8

bride's presence in the bathroom, took it into his head to burst joyously in upon her.

I've tried many times to interpret the scene as it must have presented itself to his eyes. Bearing in mind that he hadn't grasped the function of my gift in the first place, all he registered was this stranger wearing a rubber shower-cap pulled down over his eyes, kneeling in front of Bernice – and creating this *rasping* noise. . . .

Well, it's all water under the bridge now and I'm not really complaining. As soon as I was considered well enough to eat solids again, Giorgio even had the generosity to send me a box of fruit jellies. But what's beyond all doubt is this: as far as moving in on the Fun People is concerned, I've blown all chances.

In fact, I doubt if my name is even acknowledged by any of them any more. If I'm ever mentioned at all, it's only by the fun-soubriquet Giorgio used in addressing his jellies – 'Lo zotico que limó'.

Don't bother getting out the Italian dictionary. The translation is etched upon my cortex:

'The Lout That Filed.'

Let us now praise famous men, and the fathers that begat us

Ecclesiasticus xliv. 1

I answered the front door one evening and there stood a thinnish, faintly familiar figure.

"Yes?" I said.

"It's me!" said the figure. "Nicholas. Nicholas Menon. Husband of Carol. Your vicar."

I peered. "So it is! Come in, old friend!"

I persuaded him to accept a glass of herbal mixture – the juice of juniper berries, distilled, with ice and lemon and not too much tonic – and brought the conversation round to the change in his appearance.

"You used to be thick, Nick," I said, groping for tactful words. "But you've lost a lot of weight. You're now, how can I put it, a slicker vicar. What pared away the pounds? A diet? Dietary biscuits? A cellular wafer?"

"A glandular fever. But herein lies my problem. My clothes are now four sizes too large and I am to officiate at a wedding tomorrow."

"As indeed I know," I answered warmly. "The *Staines and Egham News* is my bible. Sunninghill Parish Church. Morning-suits, marquee among the rhododendrons and the cream of the *Tatler's* photographic staff."

"Even so," he said. "Now, I have found one suit that fits me, a clerical grey number from my student days which was lagging the church boiler, and I have taken it to the cleaners in Virginia Water. They assure me that it will be ready for collection just before I have to set out for the wedding tomorrow."

"Well, that should do the trick, Nick." I replied. "Wherein lies your problem?"

"The manager of the cleaners has just telephoned to say that his pressing machine has expired in a cloud of steam. My suit will be cleaned, spun in a drum until dry, but, alas, not pressed."

"Ah!" I said. "So you either officiate tomorrow looking like Stan Laurel wearing Oliver Hardy's suit, or wearing a suit straight out of the spin-dryer, wrinkled like a walnut."

"There seems no other choice."

I mixed us another half-litre of herbal comfort.

"Timings?" I asked.

"Collect suit, 2.30. Drive back to Thorpe Vicarage and change at great speed. Arrive at the church at 2.50. I can just do the journey in 16 minutes – Carol timed me yesterday with the kitchen plinger."

I am a firm believer in Lateral Thinking in problems like these. So I assumed a Lateral position on the carpet and gave myself up to Thought. After, I suppose, some nine minutes I sat up.

"We will be waiting for you at the cleaners tomorrow with a vehicle," I said, emphasising each word. "You will enter the vehicle, with your suit, and be driven to the church. On the way your suit will be neatly pressed – WHILE IT IS ON YOU!"

His face was a study.

There were all too few hours left for preparation, for racing round to the builder's merchants, the camping equipment shop, the iron-mongers, to say nothing of persuading Mr Marshall to lend us his Mobile Greengrocery van.

2.30 the next day saw my wife, son and I, in Mr Marshall's van, waiting outside the cleaners in Virginia Water. My wife had lit the two camping stoves and fixed the rubber tubing to the spouts of the two kettles. Jamie was keeping the engine running for a smooth getaway.

Nicholas emerged, clutching his clean but crumpled suit, and look-ing, I thought, a shade apprehensive.

Once Nick was in the van, Jamie let in the clutch and proceeded towards Sunninghill. Nick changed into his suit in a secluded corner by the cabbages and on my word of command assumed a prone position on the floor.

Rolling forward the two three-foot lengths of six-inch diameter, salt glaze pottery drainage pipes I deftly slipped them up Nick's legs. There was an awkward moment when his right shoe jammed in the pipe but a blow or two with the starting handle freed the foot and no time was lost. Polly's kettles were then on the boil and, on the word of command, she inserted the rubber tubes up the pipes.

We allowed the steam to play through the pipes for six minutes. I

11

then slid the pipes away from the legs and Nick stood up for the next stage, which consisted of applying bulldog clips so as to form creases in the damp, hot fabric. Eighty of these were clipped on, twenty to each crease, back and front, both legs. As Nick sat on the tailboard of the van, dangling his legs in the airstream to dry off his trousers, we began on the jacket.

First we removed the jacket, replacing it with a heatproof waistcoat made by my wife from eighteen oven gloves sewn together. Next we dampened the jacket with water from the watering-can Mr Marshall used to freshen up his lettuces. We then replaced the jacket on Nick, and covered the entire surface of the jacket, sleeves as well, in oven-proof aluminium foil. After checking that Nick was completely foiled, I lit my little calor-gas blow torch and began playing it carefully over the foil, keeping it moving, watching for tell-tale puffs of steam which told me that the scheme was working.

At one point Nick seemed to slump.

"Are you all right?" I enquired, anxiously. "Not the old ticker, vicar?"

But it was only some large potatoes which had fallen off a high rack, when Jamie had taken a right-hand bend at speed, and hit Nicholas on the head.

We stripped off the hot foil, held the jacket out of the window to cool it off, and the job was done.

At 2.49 precisely my son pulled up with a jerk outside the gates of Sunninghill church, a rain of assorted choice veg descended upon us, and Nick got out of the van and made his way towards the vestry door, looking smart and neat in his well-pressed suit.

He was still steaming a little here and there but we reckoned that anybody noticing it in church would assume it to be a kind of nimbus.

"Well," said my wife, plucking a brussels sprout from her hair. "Thank goodness that's over."

"Over?" I said, incredulity in my voice. "Over? It hasn't really started yet. We are on our way to our first million with the Muir On-Site Valet Van!"

"You don't really suppose you can make money with this . . . this . . ."

"Consider," I said, my voice rising with boyish enthusiasm. "It'll be the Fourth of June soon. Founder's Day at Eton. Statesmen, judges and millionaires trudging along Eton High Street, suits crumpled after sitting all day in deck-chairs watching cricket. I step out of the van, parked by the kerb. 'Touch up, my lord? Just step inside!' And then there's Henley Regatta. Hundreds of old chaps in little pink caps – Leanderthal Man – watching their sons skulling up and down and wondering how they are going to make the old blazer last through the week. 'Care for a spruce-up before your son wins the race, sir? Polly – put the kettles on!' Thank goodness that Nick started us going.''

"What are you trying to say?"

"Let us now press famous men, and the fathers at regattas!"

Discretion is the better part of valour

Proverb

I was watching a blue movie the other night – it wasn't meant to be that colour, but my TV set hasn't been the same since I turned it over on its side to watch more comfortably while lying in bed – and it was one of those wartime flying stories.

My mind immediately snapped back to that summer of 1941 when I was a Lab. Technician in the Photographic Unit of an RAF Training Station up in Northern Scotland. Our task was to teach budding Intelligence Officers how to 'read' Aerial Reconnaissance photographs. (Oh, you remember what they were – those photos of enemy terrain which were taken from a great height by our reconnaissance planes.)

My part in this training operation was boring but simple. Whenever we received an A.R. photo ('Aerial Reconnaissance'; come on now, don't make me have to explain *everything*), I would inspect it, select an appropriate square of it, blow that square up into a ten-by-eight glossy, then pass out several copies of this enlargement among the I.O.s. They would study their ten-by-eights through magnifying glasses, then each would take his turn interpreting the significant topographical features suggested by the photo: reservoirs, high ground, railway lines, wooded areas, etc.

Got the hang of it now? I hope so, because I now have to explain some of the handicaps under which I worked.

The principal one was that I never *received* any Aerial Reconnaissance photographs. Oh, Reconnaissance Command posted them to me all right, but as they were somewhere down in the Home Counties and the part of Northern Scotland we were in was really excessively Northern, the mail never reached us. Consequently I was obliged to obtain my supply of A.R. photos from whatever alternative sources I could find.

Well, at that time and in that place, there was only one alternative source – elderly back-numbers of the *National Geographic Magazine*, which the Dental Officer kept in his ante-room, presumably because anaesthetics were also in short supply. Several of these contained Aerial Photographs which were quite adequate for my purposes. As they were usually of places like The Great Barrier Reef or Popa-catapetl, I must admit the trainees didn't get that many marshalling-yards or heavy-water factories to recognise. Still, in wartime, improv-isation itself becomes a virtue.

The other handicap I had to surmount was that as, in this remote corner, there was little else but scenery available in the way of off-duty pleasures, the Station had a thriving Camera Club. This meant that every moment of my spare time was taken up in developing and printing snaps for an entire squadron of keen amateur photographers.

It was this keenness which precipitated the awkward incident. For some time, the Flight Sergeant in charge of our Cookhouse had been paying court to a crofter's daughter named Ella McGivern. The only female in twenty-five square miles, she was an unprepossessing girl with a skin like a water-biscuit and legs like two vacuum-cleaner bags. Nevertheless, because of the sheer lack of competition, she functioned as our neighbourhood sex object.

For that reason, excitement ran high when it was announced in DRO's that, on the following Friday evening, Ella had agreed to act as a live female model for the Camera Club. Fever pitch was reached when it became known, through less official channels, that the Flight Sergeant had persuaded her to pose in the nude.

In those days, of course, the word 'nude' was hardly the absolute term that it is today and Ella was insisting on retaining a pair of P.T. shorts below and a square of transparent net-curtaining up top. But when you've been the best part of eight months in a remote corner of Northern Scotland, even that is a fairly heady prospect.

Accordingly, come Friday, not only was the entire Camera Club to be seen clicking away at her but also a neighbouring platoon of Pioneer Corps, the complete intake of Intelligence Officers, all the sentries and two German parachutists.

For me, however, it meant only a virtually insuperable workload. For in addition to the task of developing single-handed all the figure studies of Ella that were snapped that evening, I also had to make ready an adequate supply of ten-by-eights for the official Aerial Photograph Interpretation Test which the C.O. had laid on for the Intelligence Officers the following morning.

The aerial photograph which I'd selected as the subject of the Test was of an area that, again, could hardly be described as a raging battleground. As time was short and the copies of the *National Geographic Magazine* were dwindling, I'd chosen a picture of a place called Karakorum, which is a mountain range in Tibet. As was my practice, I squared it off, selected an appropriate square and placed it under the enlarger.

At least, I think that's what I enlarged. To this day I can't be really sure. Bearing in mind that I also had in my Lab at the time three hundred or so Art Poses of Miss McGivern, the possibilities of error were considerable.

Mind you, the thought that I might have erred did not strike me until the following morning when the Test was already under way. I wandered in and watched the Intelligence Officers scanning their ten-by-eights of what they'd been told was 'mountain terrain'. Only then did it occur to me that what they were all studying through their magnifying glasses might, conceivably, through sheer pressure of work and lack of sleep, be a monstrous enlargement of some section of Ella McGivern.

"Excuse me, sir." I tugged at the C.O.'s sleeve. "There is a possibility I may have made a boob."

The C.O. was a man who could have given irritability lessons to Captain Bligh. "Belt up, Corporal," he said. Then, to one of the Intelligence Officers – "Come on then, Pilot Officer Lacey. Make anything of it?"

Pilot Officer Lacey nodded confidently. "It's at least five thousand feet high," he said. "And there's cart tracks leading up the lower slopes."

"There's also traces of volcanic activity," volunteered a fellow Intelligence Officer. "And is that a small hut at the top?"

I could not, in all conscience, allow this to go on. I leant towards the C.O's ear and quietly confessed the possibility that I had submitted an error. Equally quietly he reduced me to AC2 and confined me to camp until 1957.

Then he turned to the officers. "I'm afraid the Test must be aborted, gentlemen," he said. "A certain measure of uncertainty has arisen regarding its subject matter."

With some distaste, he picked up a ten-by-eight. Surveying it, he said:

"This creation is Tibet, or part of Ella."

There's many a slip 'twixt the cup and the lip

Proverb

France

PARIS was baking hot that May in 1863. The sun shone down, the temperature went up, tempers frayed, farmers prayed, the level of the Seine dropped, a revival of Gluck's opera *Iphigenia in Aulis* flopped, Sarah Bernhardt made her debut, people walking past drains went 'Pheew!', and the pavements were hot enough to *flamber* a crêpe-suzette on.

Idlers of the town strolling past Maxim's restaurant, picking their way carefully over the kneeling chefs and the suzettes, could only envy the rich courtesans who clip-clopped past in their open carriages, the moving air cooling their brows and disturbing such traces of lovely hair as escaped from beneath their characteristic, egg-shaped hats (*oeufs en cocottes*).

At a table in the Café de Bade, Émile Zola tried to stop the sweat dropping off his chin onto his manuscript as he put the finishing touches to his searing exposé of slavery in the banana plantations, *Nana*.

In a cheap bistro, a gaunt unhappy-looking English painter of draperies, by the name of Jack Hughes, put a paper doily on his head, balanced a silver sugar-sifter on top, puffed out his cheeks and said "Look everybody – Queen Victoria!" Few of his laughing fellow-artists guessed that his ambition was to become a leading Impressionist.

Perhaps the coolest spot in all Paris was beneath the great trees of the Bois de Boulogne. And it was there, in the very heart of the Bois, that the painter Édouard Manet was making his final attempt to win recognition. As he told his friends, "If the public does not like this last picture of mine, I shall do myself, as the English say, in."

It was a beautiful setting for a painting. Manet had erected his easel in the shadow of a huge pile of granite boulders known to Parisians as

Lover's Leap. There was grass, and trees, and in the background a pond full of carp which blew bubbles and swam about and did whatever mysterious things carp do to while away the time.

The picture was to be called '*Déjeuner sur l'herbe*' (Lunch is on Herbie), and was to depict Herbie giving a picnic lunch to a friend and a couple of girls. All of them nude. The nudity was partly to give the picture a neo-classical appeal but mostly because Manet was hopeless at painting dresses and pairs of trousers.

And so Manet painted furiously, while his mistress, Suzanne, and three friends sat with nothing on and tried to keep still.

"Herbie!" cried Manet, suddenly. "You're the host. You're supposed to be lolling at ease, chatting Suzanne. Why have you turned on to your left side?"

"Boil on me bum".

Manet muttered a Gallic imprecation.

More painting. Then:

"Ow!" from Suzanne. "Ow! Cor! Ow!"

"Now what?" from Manet.

"Ants! In the pants. Or where the pants would be if I was wearing any. Which thanks to you I'm not." She jumped up and danced about.

Manet gritted his teeth in exasperation. "I don't know why I keep you on as a model" he muttered.

"I do," she muttered back, "judging from last night."

"What was that?"

"Nothing. Nothing."

More painting. Then Manet flung his brush down in exasperation.

"You, girl, whatever your name is!" he bellowed. "You're supposed to be reclining on one elbow on the grass. What are you doing back there in the pond?"

"Paddling!" she bellowed back. "Got a bunion. It's hard on a girl's feet in my profession."

Somehow, just one day before the picture had to be entered for the Salon, it was finished. Manet sent for his friend, Émile Zola, and waited, trembling, for his verdict.

"Sorry, Éd," said Zola, shaking his head sadly. "You have here a stinkeroo. A floperoo *formidable* (formidable). It's the nudes, old lad. Everybody's painted them this year. Nudes bathing, nudes up trees, nudes chasing each other round urns. Another nude painting doesn't stand a snowflake in hell's chance. Disappointing, I know, but I'm sure you want me, your old friend Zola, to be realistic."

Manet went white, including his ginger beard. "But there is no time to paint another!" he whispered. "And I can't paint clothes on to the figures – I can't DO clothes! This is *rideaux* (curtains) for me. Be so kind as to hand me that poison-bottle marked 'Poison' . . ."

"Wait!" cried Zola. "There must be a way . . ." He strode up and down for a while. Then he lifted a clenched fist to the ceiling and cried in a great voice, "*J'accuse! J'accuse!*" (Jack Hughes! Jack Hughes!)

"It is a name I have heard . . ."

"He is a gaunt, unhappy English painter who gives impersonations of Queen Victoria. But he is, my friend, a Drapery Man! You know, do you not, how those execrable English society portrait painters work? They paint in only the hands and the face and then engage a Drapery Man to paint in the clothes. Some hack like – Jack Hughes!"

The colour began to suffuse back into Manet's beard. "Suzanne!" He commanded. "Put some clothes on and fetch Jack Hughes!"

It was arranged within the hour. For the sum of ten francs, cash in advance, Hughes agreed to clothe the four figures in the painting.

"A nice pink dress for the girl paddling in the pond, if I might make a suggestion, sir," he said. "And a modish green muslin for the foremost bird. For the two gents I would suggest dark jackets and light trousers. With a smoking hat complete with tassel for the lad in the foreground." And he left.

Alas, how often in the history of Hope has the goblet been dashed from the lips before a drop of liquor had graced tonsil?

Hughes bought a bottle of absinthe with the ten francs and in three hours was as stewed as an eel. He managed to paint clothes on to the two men, but the paddling girl was left in what looked like a white underslip, and Suzanne was, as she usually was, stark naked. His landlady delivered the picture to the Salon.

Manet slipped into the Exhibition Hall the following night, but he only got as far as the door. The howls of rage and anger from the critics jostling round his picture were enough. He went very white, Whiter than white. And slipped away into the Paris night.

It's a pity he did not stay, really. An hour later a remarkable change had come over the gallery. Word had spread round the city that there was a beastly, degrading picture in the Salon and a hundred thousand excited art lovers were trying to batter their way in. And the artists of Paris had decided that Manet was an important pioneer in modern art, daring to combine classical nudes with fully-clothed figures in a contemporary setting.

20

Zola went round to Manet's studio to congratulate him, only to be met by a sobbing Suzanne. He put his arms round her to comfort her, and patted her.

"There, there, my dear," he said, "And, if you will permit an old friend, perhaps there?"

"Édouard has gone!" she sobbed, nodding. "He came in, asked for his poison-bottle marked 'Poison' and rushed out again!"

Together they searched Paris. But nowhere did they find any trace of a pale-faced painter with a ginger beard carrying a poison-bottle.

"There is one tiny hope left," wheezed Zola as they climbed back up to Montmartre. "Put some clothes on, then we'll try the Bois de Boulogne. There's just a chance that he returned to the spot where he painted his picture."

And so they crept through the dark wood towards the little patch of grass between the granite bluff and the pond. Suzanne made Zola go on ahead, because of what he might find there.

What he found was a familiar figure, supine on the turf, motionless, clutching a small bottle. But not a poison-bottle marked 'Poison'. It was a quarter-bottle marked 'vin ordinaire'. And the figure was gently snoring.

Zola retraced his steps back to where Suzanne was anxiously waiting. "He grabbed the wrong bottle", he said.

"Then –" she cried, "he has not done himself, as he has so frequently threatened to, in?"

"Indeed no," said Zola, pivoting her until she was facing the horizontal genius –

"There's Manet. Asleep. 'Twixt the carp and the Leap."

A stitch in time saves nine

Proverb

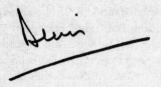

LOOKING back on my literary career, I think the most fulfilling period was when I was writing the Society Column for the *Barbers' and Hairdressers' Quarterly*. Although the work brought me into contact with most of the leading people in the trade, the one who has lingered longest in my memory is old Dino Goldoni.

A small, balding man, with a face like a melancholy knee-cap, he ran The Short Sharp Shave Shop, a two-chair lock-up off Camden Town High Street. His establishment owed its name to the fact that Dino, a three-time winner of the Masters Shaving Competition sponsored annually by my publication, had retired as undisputed champion of the art.

Now, however, he had received a challenge. A new man, a Greek called Andreas, whose saloon in Kensal Rise was the first to feature a basin into which you leaned *backwards* for a shampoo, had challenged Dino to a Shave Off.

For those of you unfamiliar with the rules of this contest, a Shave Off is a sudden-death competition in which two barbers vie with each other to see which can shave the most people over a given ten-minute period, any severed eyebrow or ear counting as two faults.

Old Dino, as the holder of three Golds, was fairly indulgent about the event at first. In the preceding week, he did put in a little practice on his backscrape, using as target his customary assistant, an Irishman called No Nose McGinty, but such was his confidence he spent little more than an hour a day at wrist-flexing and lather-rubbing. I must admit that I too regarded the occasion as no more than a work-out for Dino, even wondering a little at Andreas' temerity.

On the day of the Shave Off, however, my eyes were opened. As

usual a guest-manicurist had been brought in to act as Official Starter –
in this case, a very popular girl called Florence, known throughout the
trade as Cash Flo. My Editor and a man from the board of Silvikrin
were along as judges. But just as Flo was about to drop the hot towel –
the time-honoured signal for the start – Dino let out a startled yell.
"Where's-a my brush? Who's-a swipe my brush?"

To the layman, the most important item of equipment in this kind
of event would appear to be the razor. Not so. In competition shaving,
the brush is all. Over years of use a barber will have moulded it to his
individual hand, rendered it smooth and swift, learned just how much
pressure to apply going round corners and across the cheekbone.

Now, at the crucial moment, Dino's brush had disappeared. When
Andreas stepped forward smirking, I realised how dangerously we had
underestimated him. Noting that he was clad, not in the grey overall
of the old school, but in one of the new-fangled white nylon smocks, I
reminded myself of the old adage: beware of Greeks wearing shifts.

"I claim a walkover", Andreas said with a white nylon smile. My
Editor cocked an enquiring eye at Dino. He spread his hands miserably,
acknowledging defeat.

"One moment, please," I said. "May I respectfully remind you of
the BBC rules?" My Editor frowned but I held my ground. According
to the official body which has established the conventions for these
events, the British Barbers' Committee, if a competitor loses an item
of equipment, he is allowed fifteen minutes to replace it before being
disqualified.

"Very well," said the Editor. "You have a quarter-of-an-hour." He
started his stopwatch.

Dino shook his head hopelessly. "What's-a good?" he said (or
possibly "What's a-good?"). "How'm I gonna find a good brush
round these-a parts in fifteen minutes?"

"Listen," I said. "These-a parts are Camden Town. Right on the
door-step of the London Zoo. Do you shave any of the keepers there?"

"My best customers," Dino said with a flash of the old pride. "They
all-a come to Dino."

"Right," I replied. "Then we get on to the Head Keeper."

"What for do I need a Head Keeper?"

"Because it's a question of keeping your head. Seeing that there's no
time to skin a badger, what's the next best animal for making a soft
pliable shaving-brush?" When Dino shrugged in bewilderment, I
pressed on urgently. "Ostrich feathers! The tail-feathers of an ostrich."

"He's-a not gonna pull all-a the feathers off his best ostrich just-a because Dino –"

"We're not asking him to," I interrupted. "Tell him to bring the ostrich itself along. Preferably a docile one."

Dino sighed and moved to the phone. It did take a certain amount of explaining on his part and roughly the same amount of expostulating on mine but, praise be, no more than twelve minutes had elapsed when the door opened and a tall sun-tanned man entered, leading an amiably-visaged ostrich.

I had a piece of twine ready waiting. It was the work of a moment to tie it round the ostrich's tail-feathers, pulling them tight so that they formed one uniform, manageable plume. As my Editor's fingers moved to his stop-watch knob to signal the end of our quarter-of-an-hour's grace, the plume was completed.

Down went Flo's hot-towel, and the contest was on. Into the shaving-mug went the plume, on to the customer's face went the lather – Dino was off and away.

Today, wherever men with cut-throats foregather, they still talk about Dino's performance that afternoon. Up till then, the world record for the ten-minute Shave Off had been seven customers. Dino did not simply break that record, he shattered it. The new figure he established still stands.

As I mentioned earlier, in terms of emotional experience it was one of the most fulfilling episodes of my life. Whenever the bad times come now, or the old fire flickers, I still summon up remembrance of the phrase I headlined my story with:

"Ostrich And Twine Shaves Nine."

A jug of wine, a loaf of bread – and thou

Omar Khayyám
'*Rubaiyat*'

Frank

WELL, Jeremy, I understand from your aunty that you are going to be married to that nice girl in the gas showroom. No, I wouldn't agree that she is all that enormous. A little bulky, perhaps, particularly when she is demonstrating an oven, but no doubt once safely married she will moderate her present enthusiasm for eating things like chocolate fudge and cold roast potatoes.

How wise you are to get your ferrets used to new sleeping quarters; I think you should consider moving them right out of your bedroom now that they have got used to not sleeping in your bed.

Faintly on the same theme, I have a word of warning to you. It has been said that a bride's attitude towards her betrothed can be summed up in three words: Aisle. Altar. Hymn. You must prepare to resist alteration in those areas where a change is not an improvement.

It may come as a shock to you when you are married so perhaps now is the time to prepare yourself mentally to face a generally acknowledged fact; most women have an eccentric attitude towards personal hygiene.

For instance, women tend to underestimate, some of them by weeks, how long a pair of socks can be worn before they need to be changed.

Brides also fail to appreciate that when a man's hands become soiled, say through dismantling a carburettor or shifting a heap of coal, Dame Nature has provided absorbent matter for him to wipe his hands on in the shape of drying-up cloths, bathroom towels, and the edges of table-cloths. You will find that this natural practice will be frowned upon.

But much more important, and in some cases downright dangerous, is the feminine insistence that the male should wallow in a hot bath at least once a week.

The bath is not a British thing, Jeremy. Like a lot of other things, such as polo, cats, markets and carpets, it was imported from ancient Persia. However, the Persian version had an additional attraction; it was mixed bathing.

The bath next cropped up in ancient Greece. Mrs Archimedes used to fill her husband's bath right up to the brim. Archimedes found that the water slopped over the sides when he jumped in, and by weighing the amount of water spilt, and weighing himself, he discovered a formidable argument against baths, or at least full ones, in that a floating body displaces its own weight of water. He also discovered that the displaced water wet the bath-towel and made it so heavy that when he hung it on the towel-rail it pulled out the nails and the rail fell off the wall. So he invented the screw.

The idea of washing one's person seems to have been introduced into England during the reign of Henry II by a cleric of advanced views who used to give himself an all-over wash in a pail. He became known as Thomas O'Bucket.

The full obsession with immersing the body in the alien element came into fruition in Victorian times. They had a motto then, 'Cleanliness is Next to Godliness' – a sentiment about as logical as 'Lawn-mowing is Next to Madrigal-Singing'.

Consider the matter from a scientific point of view. Your skin is like a Fair Isle sweater (yours more than most people's, Jeremy, but I am sure the blotches are mostly due to nerves). Think of yourself as entirely covered in a kind of knitted garment which keeps your bones in place. It has neat edging round the lips to stop your mouth from fraying, and has some loose embroidery on top which we call hair. And like a Fair Isle sweater, it is a living, breathing thing, full of natural oils. Now if you soak this continually in hot water, and rub it all over with a cake of chemical substance made from rancid grease boiled up with caustic soda, then the natural protective oils will be washed away and all sorts of things will happen, beginning with colds and chills and ending with the skin shrinking, moisture getting in and, eventually, rusty ribs.

My own plan for personal cleanliness is simplicity itself and entirely in concord with nature.

Once a week – or so – stand naked in the bath and dab yourself lightly all over with a bit of cotton wool moistened in rainwater. Don't use tapwater, which has chemicals and impurities in it to make it taste nice. Keep an old jug handy and stick it under a drain pipe, or the down pipe of a gutter, so that you have a supply of rainwater always to hand.

Areas of mud, axle-grease, dried paint, and tar should be given individual treatment with a loofah. Not a wet loofah, which is flabby and useless, but a dry loofah. Scrub away hard until the offending matter is dislodged, pausing only if you find that you are about to draw blood.

For a final toning up, rub yourself down with a slice of stale bread, using a circular motion and no butter. Bread has the property of absorbing water and grease, and erasing any pencil marks you might have overlooked.

Dash about a bit on the bathroom lino to dry off and the job is done, using pure, natural means.

So, Jeremy, take a firm stand on the question of frequent hot baths, which are foreign, pagan, and dangerous. All your bride needs for a clean and decent husband is four things:

A jug of rain, a loofah, bread – and thou.

He who hesitates is lost

Proverb

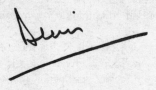

THOSE Kung Fu entertainments are an intriguing blend of bone-fracture and sententiousness. I was watching one the other night where the hero – a right prosy beggar, but the owner of a lethal left leg – observed to the baddie, "The man who loves unhappily will never finish first in the obstacle-race of Life." Then he kicked him in the groin and rode off into the commercial.

His remark, however, stayed with me. "Could that possibly account for it?" I mused. "Could that explain my own failure to break Life's tape ahead of the field?" For when I catalogue the various romantic attachments which have decorated my days – nights were generally out of the question, they had to wash their hair – the list does emerge as a pretty miserable series of encounters.

It's possibly because I started off on the wrong foot, if that's the correct anatomical referent in these matters. My adolescence, you see, was too early for what's become known as the sexual revolution. In fact, when I was seventeen, there appeared to be a sexual cease-fire. True, a roped-off section of the lending library called 'Modern' Novels offered the odd inflammatory chapter-ending, but you had to be twenty-five before you could borrow one and even then it was two old-pence per day. And when I did once manage to nail a book called *Learn to Love*, it turned out to be the sixth volume of a set of encyclo-paedias, the next volume being *Luana to Membrane*.

So, with no Dr Reuben or Martin Cole around to direct our urges, what the panting young oicks of my era adopted as behaviour-models were the sentimental Hollywood films of that period. I grew to man-hood fully believing that all girls shut their eyes when kissed on the lips, most of them standing on tiptoe with one leg bent upwards. And, at my most impressionable period, a scene in one of those films – a Charles Boyer/Jean Arthur romance – left an absolutely indelible imprint.

I can see that scene now. They were dining in a fashionable restaurant and, coffee having arrived, Boyer beckoned. A strolling violinist entered the scene and, leaning over Jean Arthur, he softly played their particular our-tune into her left ear. And as she listened, her hand involuntarily stole across the table and her little finger linked into his. (Into Charles Boyer's I mean. Had it been the violinist's, it would, of course, have cocked-up the melody-line utterly.)

Well, I can't tell you to what heights of dewy-eyed soppiness that moment sent me. To the sort of male I was then – and, if truth be told, have been ever since as well – all of romance was in that scene. "If only," I thought, "if only I could arrange an identical set-up for myself, Life need strew no other rose in my path."

For more than one reason it wasn't easy. Snag A was that no restaurant in my postal district featured a strolling musician; Snag B, there was no girl I fancied anywhere near strongly enough to buy a whole meal for. However, within a month both A and B were taken care of.

First, right next door, a new family moved in containing an eminently molestable daughter called Lily. For the statistically-minded, her measurements were 36, 24, 36, 27; the last figure being her I.Q. But so besotted was I by the other three numerals I cared not. The other happy circumstance was that the haberdashers in the High Street closed down and reopened – after some initial difficulties with the spelling of the neon sign – as 'The Hendon Brasserie'. More important, it was owned and personally managed by an ex-member of Bram Martin's Orchestra. Anticipating the imminent demise of the Big Bands, he had decided to invest his savings in something less transitory.

So I had it all going for me – the place, the girl, the strolling violinist. Getting Lily to agree to 'date' me, as the operation was then called, proved easier than I had anticipated and when she met me at the Brasserie she looked a knock-out. Admittedly she appeared to be about two foot taller than when I'd last seen her but that was because of the hairdo that girls of that day adopted for formal occasions – a sort of black-gloss beehive. She proved to have a healthy appreciation of food so there was little conversation through the three-course table d'hôte, Lily being occupied in stuffing herself like an out-of-work taxidermist. But when coffee was finally served, she pushed away from the table and looked at me for the first time. Taking it to be a good augury that she was still breathing quite heavily, I moved in closer. "What's your favourite tune?" I asked, giving her the Franchot Tone turned-down-on-one-side smile.

As I mentioned earlier, she was a bit hard of thinking so there was quite a pause before the answer. "I beg yours?" she said.

"Your favourite tune."

"Oh, I'm not all that musical really." She pondered. "What's the one that goes –" and she hummed a few bars.

"That's the National Anthem," I said. "Tell you what, I'll pick one." And beckoning the manager-violinist over, I said "Listen, my good fellow. Can you play 'Time After Time I Tell Myself That I'm'?"

He nodded and winked. Then, leaning forward to Lily's ear, he began – on that low, sexy string they hardly ever seem to use any more. I locked my eyes into Lily's and awaited developments. She was still blowing a bit but, sure enough, after no more than a half-chorus, her hand came creeping across the table.

As I found out afterwards, it was only groping for a toothpick, but no matter. I seized her little finger, curled my own little finger into it, gripped tight, and closed my eyes in bliss. Pure and unalloyed bliss.

In fact, so utter was the bliss that when the music ceased playing, I didn't even notice it at first. It was only when I heard a strange kind of *sawing* noise. . . .

He'd somehow got his violin-bow stuck right through her beehive! Remember how peculiarly unyielding the lacquer was that girls used in those days? If you ever ran your fingers through their hair you stood a fair chance of breaking your nails. Well, this clown, this poop, he'd managed to push his bow right into the interior. And now the resin had somehow *bonded* itself to . . . oh, it was just so dispiriting, so awful, I can't even bear recalling any more of it.

Anyway, when that's the kind of foot a fellow gets started off on in the romance line, you do see how miserably his later liaisons are going to turn out. And so it proved. That's why that line of Kung Fusion set me brooding so much. "The man who loves unhappily will never finish first in the obstacle-race of Life."

Or, if you prefer the Western version:

"He who has sad dates is last."

None was for a party; all were for the state

Lord Macaulay
Lays of Ancient Rome: 'Horatius'

Frank

THE only bit of Spanish I remember after wrestling with it for a term at school is an ancient proverb which went: 'Whoever Spitteth at Heaven Shall Have it Fall Back in his Eye.' A good thought; cautionary, ballistically sound. And it seems to me that we should have a similar proverb in English to warn the impulsive of the dangers of doing the opposite; not spitting at Heaven but trying to get a bit nearer to it. I propose the following: 'Whoever Foolishly Attempteth to Bring About a Social Reform Very Likely will Find that it Falleth Upon Cloth Ears and Lo the Ground Will be Stony and Before He Knoweth Where He is He Will be Back Where He Started having Achieved Sweet Fanny Adams and Made to Feel an Utter Nana.'

That's only a first draft, of course. It will need honing before it goes into *The Oxford Dict. of Eng. Proverbs*.

The need for such a proverb was brought home to me recently when I attempted to set on its way a small but, it seemed to me, vital social reform.

The Classless Society is the dearest wish of all of us but spreading the word that beans-on-toast are chic and Rolls-Royces are heavy on brake-linings is only nibbling at the problem. There is one real bastion of class-consciousness which must be removed.

Until recently the main Class giveaways were speech and dress. If somebody spoke a little too loudly, with a pre-war BBC announcer's accent, keeping the vowels well open, then he or she was an Upper. If all this was attempted and it just failed, then he or she was a Middle. Mumbling mangled vowels, and local colour in the accent indicated Lower. But nowadays, thanks to telly, pop-music, and the media generally, our youth and our trendier middle-aged now talk what might be termed Standard Received Disc-Jockey. If you meet a lad in Windsor High Street it is now no longer possible to tell from his speech whether he is Eton or Slough Comprehensive.

Clothes have also ceased to be reliable indicators of Class. If you spot a little riot of colour ambling along the King's Road it could well be the rhythm guitarist of The Who. It could also be The Right Hon. Leo Abse M.P. on his way to the opening of Parliament.

But there is still one infallible way of separating the sheep from the lambs, the ewes from the non-ewes, and that is what we call the place where we all, from time to time, are compelled to go. Roughly speaking, Uppers go to the Lavatory, Middles to the Loo and Lowers go to the Toilet.

This is oversimplifying the picture to an enormous extent; in fact, the situation is in a state of flux. Loo is holding its own fairly well but there is a strong, perhaps 14%, swing to Toilet and most of these gains are at the expense of Lavatory.

These terms are totally non-interchangeable in society. Uppers and Middles recoil from the vulgarity of the word 'Toilet'. Uppers and Lowers both regard 'Loo' as being a hopelessly twee euphemism. And Lowers and Middles join in finding the aristocratic use of the word 'Lavatory' utterly disgusting.

Now it wouldn't be too bad if we had just those three words – the U.S.A. manages happily with two, the John and the Can – but unfortunately we have a great many more words for the Unmentionable Thing. Consequently when strangers meet in an English house, and nature calls, our society breaks into a *mille-feuille* of social strata, the guest trying frantically to sort out in his mind which euphemism his host is most likely to embrace and the host similarly trying to fit euphemism to guest.

Many older hosts and hostesses, who grew up in a protected, non-permissive society, can't bear to apply any word at all to It. They say, "Would you like to . . . (faint upward wave of right hand). . . ?" Or simply, "Are you . . . all right?"

School-children are brought up to avoid a confrontation by being taught to use such evasions as "Please, Miss, may I be excused?" "Please, Sir, may I leave the room?" The confusion which this produces in the delicate, growing mind is illustrated by the small boy who suddenly put his hand up and said "Please, Miss, Johnny's left the room on the floor".

Keen euphemismaticians often study a stranger's house for clues before taking the plunge. Framed prints of vintage cars on the walls, pewter tankards, and "Match of the Day" on the telly indicate an approach along the lines of:

"Where's the geography, old son?" Or:

"Excuse me, but I must go and see whether my horse has kicked off its blanket".

(*Note:* These phrases are rarely necessary as this host invariably greets his guests with a cheerful, "By the way, the bog's on the landing".)

Colour Supplements lying about, Hi-Fi, and Spanish Claret indicate a slightly more roguish approach from the host:

"Ah – if anyone needs the House of Lords it's at the end past the au-pair's room." Or:

"Comforts anyone?"

And in between these phrases there are a hundred others, each one clung to by a section of the population as being the one socially acceptable phrase which will protect them from hideous embarrassment.

Obviously something must be done to straighten this situation out, and the answer to the problem is to find a word for the Thing which is acceptable to all ranks. But which word? 'Lavatory' is useless; it is the word plumbers use for a washbasin. 'Toilet' is a horrid euphemism, imported from the U.S.A., which really means a lady's dressing-table. 'Loo' doesn't mean anything at all, being a hangover from eighteenth-century Edinburgh when folks were wont to empty their chamber pots out of the top stories of tenement buildings with a cheerful warning cry of, "Guardy-loo!"

The problem was solved for me one evening when a small, round, innocent face looked up into mine and said, simply, "I want potty". It wasn't a child who spoke, in fact, it was a shortish Rural Dean who had come round about a subscription and had stayed to bash the sherry. But the simple, child's word 'Potty' was the word I had been searching for. An old, honourable, easily remembered word, and the only word of the whole bunch which described the Thing itself.

My mind went immediately into overdrive (unhappily, I recall, forgetting the Rural Dean and his pressing problem) and it seemed to me that I should form a society to promote the use of the word 'Pot'. Perhaps calling the society Pioneers of Truth (thus making clever use of the initial letters), with myself as (paid) President. Perhaps I would write the society a brief, expensive manifesto. . . .

I saw the Rural Dean out of the front door and into the bushes and immediately sat down and wrote out a questionnaire, to send to a hundred people to test whether I had judged the people's mood correctly. I asked them to state clearly whether they would be in favour of everybody settling to call the Thing something like 'Potty' rather than messing about pretending that they were nipping outside to check whether the trusty steed had kicked off its saddle.

It was when the results of my referendum were all in that I realised a sad truth. A truth encapsulated in the proverb 'Whoever Foolishly Attempteth to Bring About a Social Reform Very Likely Will Find that it Falleth Upon Cloth Ears . . . (etc.)' The figures were conclusive:

None was for a Potty; all were for The Steed.

The rank is but the guinea's stamp

Robert Burns
'For a' that and a' that'

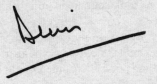

YES, I've had some odd experiences in Gents' Loos – I still chuckle at what happened when I used the one in the Leaning Tower of Pisa – but the oddest, I think, occurred behind the door marked 'Maharajahs' at a certain well-known Indian restaurant in Mayfair.

Immediately upon entering its marble vastness, my attention was caught by the behaviour of a tall, red-headed gentleman. Standing in front of a mirror, he was inspecting himself keenly, all the while nodding his head rapidly up and down, then shaking it equally forcefully to and fro. After watching his vigorous nodding-and-shaking for some several minutes, I could no longer restrain my curiosity. "Excuse me, sir," I said. "Are you in the throes of some deep internal conflict?"

"I fear my dilemma is of a more external nature," he replied. "I am endeavouring to ascertain just how far – look, sir, perhaps you can enlighten me." Performing some further agitations of his head, he asked, "When I go like this, do you chance to notice any marked alteration of my visage?"

I gazed at him intently. Finally, "Yes." I replied. "Your forehead appears to – diminish."

He sighed heavily. "As I feared," he said. Then seating himself upon the chinchilla top of the used paper towel basket, he told me his story.

At a very early age he had had the misfortune to lose his hair. Not all of it, but enough to impart to his scalp in adult life a kind of see-through look. It had rendered him acutely, and perhaps unduly, sensitive about his appearance; to such an extent that he had, as far as was possible, shunned all contact with the opposite sex.

As he was a gynaecologist by trade, such a withdrawal had proved as damaging professionally as it was socially. However, quite recently a patient's husband had drawn his attention to a startling advance in masculine embellishment: the false hairpiece, or toupée. On impulse he had purchased one – a red one – and after trying it on, he adjudged his appearance so enhanced that he took courage in both hands and joined a mixed pot-holing group.

There, while descending a narrow chimney, he had found himself sitting on the nose of an extremely pleasing younger lady. Their acquaintanceship had ripened and now, after some months of courtship, he had invited her here to this caravanserai of curry with the express purpose of asking her to become his wife.

"And does she know about your false roof?" I broke in at this point. "Have you told her that you are, as it were, carrying on business under an assumed mane?"

He shook his head mournfully – causing another slight subsidence of the thatch. "I have not yet summoned up courage," he said. "That is why what happened during the dessert course was so dismaying. I had chosen the Gooseberry Compôte and when she asked me whether she could have my glacé cherry, I nodded my head. As I did so, suddenly I felt this unaccustomed current of air upon my cranium."

"It fell off?" Involuntarily my voice rose, for there can be few mental images more chilling than that of an upside-down red toupée in a plate of stewed gooseberries.

"Fortunately no. But it did make a significant skid forward. Happily she didn't notice, being fully occupied with her Rum Baba. So, making a trumped-up excuse, I hastened here. And now – well, now every movement seems to loosen it further. See?" He made a nodding movement again, causing another manifestation of what astronomers call, I believe, the Red Shift. "What's happened, you see, is something for which I have only myself to blame. You must understand that these things are held firm to the head by means of a strip of sticking-plaster which one is supposed to renew daily. Tonight though, such was my excitement, I neglected to effect the renewal. In consequence, unless I can now find some other means of adhesion, it's – farewell, Rozella!"

"Is that what you call it?" I asked.

"That's the young lady's name. Sir, can you perhaps suggest something by which I may anchor it?"

"Well, if all you need is a sticking-plaster, surely that First Aid

Cabinet on the wall, the one with the minarets? Something in there –?"

"I have already searched it. It has everything but sticking-plaster. Bandages, lint, iodine – even splints."

"Bandages!" I said. "What about going back with your head covered in bandages? Say that on your way here, some indigent immigrant mugged you for your lighter fuel."

"One can hardly propose in a turban. Especially not in an Indian restaurant. Have you not, perhaps, something about your person?"

I explored my pockets. "Nothing I'm afraid. Tell you what, though. In my brief-case I've got some drawing-pins. Couldn't we try to . . . no, perhaps not. What's really needed is some kind of adhesive substance, isn't it. Look, I say, here's a thought. Suppose you go back to the table and tell the waiter you've gone off the idea of stewed gooseberries, you really fancy a baked apple. Then when he brings it, you fetch it in here. Baked apple, you see, always has that toffee-bit on top. Sometimes that's of quite startling stickiness."

"But won't Rozella question my reason for taking a baked apple into the Gentlemen's Toilet?"

"Let her. In any relationship there have to be certain areas of privacy. Mind you –"

"What?"

"I don't think Indian restaurants serve baked apple."

His face, which had brightened, fell again. "Don't despair," I said. "Not yet." I hardened my eyes and gazed upwards, a habit I have when concentrating. "No use staring at the ceiling, boy," my old Maths Master used to say. "You won't find the answer up there." It never crossed his mind that I'd sneaked in the night before and scribbled out the Trig. tables all round the light fitting.

The ceiling! Wait a minute, when was it? Last Christmas? Yes! The pennies! Ten pound in pennies!

"Just wait here," I said to my toupéed friend and hurried out. Within three minutes I was back. "Ever been in a pub that's collecting for a favourite charity?" I panted. "They stick the pennies you contribute up on the ceiling. Know how? With *this*!" And I held up the bottle of stout I'd purchased from the off-licence down the street. "So if we just pour out a little, then moderately dampen the inside of your wig with it. . . ."

Two months later a small box came through my letter-box. Inside was a rather stingy piece of wedding cake.

Since that evening, I never see an advert for those hirsute artifices without recalling my friend's last-minute repair job and I wonder whether other users of hairpieces ever find themselves relying upon a similar emergency fixative. I hope not. For how precariously perched must such crowning glories be, when – in Burns' phrase –

"Their anchor's but the Guinness damp".

O, for the wings, for the wings of a dove

Mendelssohn
'Hear My Prayer'

Frank

THERE has been a lot of loose talk going on in places where thinking men congregate, like the fruit-machine salon at the Athenaeum Club and the House of Commons Sauna and Massage Parlor, as to why Britain has declined to the status of a second-class power.

Ignoring for a moment the fact that many of us see nothing disastrous in this – dropping from being Top Dog, with all the duties and responsibilities which go with it, to being Number Two can be a merciful release, as many a husband knows – the reason for this supposed decline in Britain's might seems to be in doubt. Various reasons have been advanced.

On the global level my researches have revealed the following: America thinks we are bankrupt. Scotland thinks we have too much money. Japan thinks we are too tall. Mr Enoch Powell thinks we are too tinted. Germany thinks our working-class doesn't work. Russia thinks our working-class is crushed by the rich. Switzerland thinks that according to her standards we haven't got any rich. The Confederation of British Industries thinks we are trapped between the Devil and the TUC.

On the more local level I have had meaningful dialogue with a retail-outlet contact; a piece of trendy jargon meaning that I spent an hour trotting behind Mercer the milkman as, whiff ablaze, he strode round the village bestowing pintas on doorsteps. According to Mercer, who has a fine ear for this sort of thing, local opinion holds that the sad state of the nation is attributable to one or more of the following reasons: they are putting fluoride in the water at Staines reservoir; the new motorway workings have fractured the pipes leading to Lyne Lane sewage farm and the stuff is leaking into the soil; there was a shortage of bees last summer; it's the rubbish on the telly.

All these might be contributory factors but the whole lot together would only add up to a temporary *cafard*, not a national decline. No, the real reason is more fundamental. In my opinion the decline of the British nation as a great power is directly connected with the decline in our consumption of boiled pudding.

It is an undeniable fact that our nation began to lose its pre-eminence at the same time as the good, old-fashioned steamed suet pudding fell into desuetude.

I am prepared to support my theory with facts. In medieval times the Englishman, be he noble or lewd, stood about five feet in height and, because vegetables were not invented until the eighteenth century, went to an early grave riddled with scurvy. So where did he get the energy to win at Agincourt? From boiled puddings. For centuries the ability of the English to consume boiled puddings was a matter of wonder to continentals. What hope had French or Spanish troops, fed on hot water with stringy bits of meat floating about in it, against our English bowmen, belts bursting with good pudding; suet to keep out the cold and damp, flour for bulk, and meat for energy?

Almost everything was shoved into the puddings to begin with; veal, pork, mutton, various interior organs of the deer, but latterly, from the eighteenth century, puddings came to be eaten more and more as puddings and were stuffed with plums or coated with jam.

At the height of the British Empire our public schools supplied a stream of splendid chaps to be administrators in those far-flung countries coloured red on the map. Straight from boarding-school they went, honking with adenoids, and after five years of digesting roly-poly puddings and figgy duffs, constipated to the eyebrows and thus impervious to dysentery.

All gone now, of course; both the red bits on the map and puddings. Since the last war puddings have been called 'sweets' and usually consist of either a mess of artificially tinted and flavoured froth, or a baleful mixture of semi-edible substances called something like Baked Caramel and Mallow Ring.

An honest worker queues up for his pud in the canteen and orders Manchester Tart. What is dumped on his plate is a wedge-shaped piece of thickish, warm cardboard lightly smeared with raspberry flavoured red lead. Hardly the sort of fodder to send him whistling back to Blast Furnace No. 2 replete and raring to go.

And then there's the Prime Minister. Flying to Moscow for a vital talk with the Soviet Premier. On the way they serve lunch. And what do they give him for pud on the plane? Half a tinned apricot resting on a bed of soggy rice. How can he stand up for us against the might of Russia with only that under his belt?

Ah, where are the puds of yesteryear? Spotted Dick; fine, crusty suet pudding studded with a galaxy of plump currants. Boiled Baby; heavy, densely-textured pudding boiled in a cloth. A characteristic soft coating, known to aficionados as 'the slime' was scraped gently off the outside before the pudding was anointed with very hot golden syrup. Figgy Duff: the Prince of Suet Puddings, very popular in the Royal Navy, both as food and for pressing into service as keel ballast, emergency anchor, or ammunition for the cannons. An inch-and-a-half slice of a good Figgy Duff weighed about three and a quarter pounds.

But I suppose what we old Figgy Duff and Boiled Baby fanciers miss most of all is that unique physical sensation which set in when one had eaten that delicious little bit too much pudding. It was like a pain, except that it wasn't a pain. The tum, which before the pudding had been soft and flexible, became tight as a drum and firm enough to crack a flea on. And an odd, charming ache, halfway between a spasm of wind and an old-fashioned twinge, made its presence felt. The medical name for it was the 'winge'. And it was the most satisfying feeling in the world.

Coming home from a restaurant or a dinner-party nowadays my wife may say something like:

"Wasn't that Apple-peel and Ginger Mousse good? I feel absolutely full." Or, "Did you like the Marinated Passion-Fruit and Marshmallow Whip? I don't think I'll need another meal for a week!"

I agree with her, of course. But in my heart of hearts I know that at that moment I am missing something; something beautiful which has gone forever. And I think to myself:

"O, for the winge, for the winge of a duff!"

In the great right of an excessive wrong

Robert Browning
'The Ring and the Book'

THERE is little point in going into the reasons why
Frank and I found ourselves running a Matrimonial Agency. It was, I
suppose, a panic attempt to restore our finances after the failure of our
first play, a sensitive social allegory about a black mermaid. But when,
after eight months' trading, our Agency still only had two clients on its
books, I was all for packing it in and turning the place into a massage
parlour. ("Everyone likes to feel kneaded" was the argument I used.)

But Frank is made of more determined stuff. "All we have to do is
show results." he said. "If we could just fix up the two we've got with
each other. . . !" And he drew from his roll-top desk the well-thumbed
dossiers of our only two supporters.

We gazed at their photographs with some gloom. The male client
was named Jack Longland – no relation, just one of those happy
coincidences. He was a slightly-built man, no more than five-foot-one
in height. The lady was one Emma Williamson, six-foot-four and a
good sixteen stone.

Surveying them side by side, even Frank's resolve wavered. "It's like
trying to mate a pram and a furniture van," he said. I felt my own
spirits droop like a wax banana in a heat wave. "I doubt whether
Henry Kissinger could bring these two together."

"We have to try," said Frank firmly and picked up the telephone. In
such circumstances, the first step is for each partner to be summoned to
the Agency and there shown a photograph of the other. If, in both
cases, the prospect pleases, then we arrange what is known in the trade
as a 'meet'.

Emma presented us with no difficulties. In her early forties – her *late*
early forties – she was far enough down the home-stretch to settle for

practically anything with the right hormones. "Twelve years now I've been on the Pill," she confided. "And if I don't get talking to somebody soon. . . ."

It was Jack who proved to be the recalcitrant partner. Possessing, like most small men, an acute sense of personal dignity, he was immediately sensitive to the disparity in their respective square footages. "Great ugly fat lump," he said when I displayed Emma's picture. "Put her in a white dress, you could show films on her."

Fortunately Frank is the type who could sell bagels to the Arab League. "Looks aren't everything, Jack," he argued. "And, anyway, beauty fades. But a big plain girl, Jack – she stays big and plain forever." It took a deal of persuasion but Jack was finally talked into accepting Emma's invitation to a whirl round the Planetarium the following Saturday afternoon.

In this, as in their subsequent get-togethers, it was Emma who made the running. She it also was who phoned in progress reports after each meeting. The first few were bleak indeed. "We spent an evening at Battersea Fun Fair," was one of her early bulletins. "In the Tunnel Of Love, he insisted on separate carriages."

On the few occasions that Jack dropped in to pay his subs, we found ourselves committed to long sessions of reassurance and rebuttal. "But she's so enormous," he'd protest. "In that lurex dress, it's like being out with a giant Brillo pad."

"Don't keep dwelling on Emma's bad points," Frank would plead. "Think *benefits*! Warmth in the winter and shade in the summer!"

Finally, against all odds, it began to happen. The first hint was an excited message from Emma. "Last night," she exclaimed, "last night he hung up on me so gently, it was almost a caress."

When Jack came into the office next morning, the change in his demeanour was unmistakable. "Well," he said, "I never thought I would but I have."

"Emma?" I asked eagerly.

He nodded and smiled slightly. "I've fallen for that mountain of womanhood."

"Oh well done, Jack," Frank said warmly. "Accept our sincere condolences for your future happiness."

"Dunno about getting that far," Jack said. A muscle in his cheek twitched. "Did you know she's also a bit mutt-and-jeff?"

Well, we were aware that Emma had a slight hearing problem but it was not something we'd emphasised, any more than a car dealer will go out of his way to show the wear on the rear tyres. "Could well put a spoke in the whole shooting-match, that could," Jack went on unhappily. "I mean, how do I set about proposing to her? If I go down on the knee and ask her, it could well happen that due to the inordinate distance between my mouth and her ears she won't hear a blind word. And I'm not going to kneel there shouting it. I don't hold with small-built men shouting."

Behind his glasses his eyes blinked miserably, giving him the appearance of an evicted owl. Frank and I exchanged glances. We had come to respect the little man's sensitivity towards his lack of tall, so we saw the need to tread carefully.

Then Frank narrowed his eyes and tapped the side of his nose at me. It was a gesture which meant, I recalled from our Paul Newman/Robert Redford games, he'd had an idea.

"Jack," he said. "Let me show you what we use to clean that light-fitting up on the ceiling." He crossed the room and opened the broom cupboard. Withdrawing from it a folding ladder, he said. "We use this. Jack, go thou and do likewise."

"Do what?"

"Take the ladder away, Jack. Take it round to Emma's flat, stand it at her side and climb to its topmost rung. Then make your proposal from there."

Jack's blinking slowed momentarily then became even more agitated. "But a gentleman can't go clambering about ladders in a lady's drawing room. What if she asks *why* I'm climbing up it?"

"Tell her – because it's there."

Frank still avers that it could have worked and it should have worked. All I know is it didn't work. Immediately we received Emma's distraught phone-call, we sped round to her basement flat. There, in the fireplace, lay Jack's limp and broken form.

I deduced instantly what had happened. After taking the ladder and measuring it against Emma's length, my suspicions were confirmed. The ladder was too long.

Jack, in his joyous haste, had rushed up it so fast he'd gone one rung too many, shot clean over her head, and landed in the fireplace. Now he lay where he had fallen:

In the grate, right off an excessive rung.

Frank

I must have been about nine at the time of the tragedy; a wiry, quiet lad, much given to solitary walks and Uncle William's Banana-Flavour Toffee.

They were long, hot summers at Broadstairs in those days. A military band played in the bandstand on the promenade, Uncle Mac performed his Minstrel Show on the beach twice daily, and the 'Perseverance', smelling excitingly of diesel oil fumes, took trippers for a sick round the bay.

All day was spent on the beach. I wore a bathing costume, bathing hat, and plimsolls from dawn to dusk, wet or fine. The costume was my pride; the acme of chic men's beachwear around the year 1929; the top half was like a vest, with horizontal hoops of maroon, and – a design featurette – large holes below the normal armholes. Then, working southwards, came an imitation belt with a rusty buckle, and a navy-blue lower half complete with a modesty skirt.

The bathing hat, which was worn at all times, was made of some intractable black rubber, possibly from old tractor inner-tubes, about a quarter of an inch thick. It had rubber ear-pieces welded on, into which the ears were supposed to repose snugly. Because I had found the hat on the beach my ears did not quite coincide and so not only was much agony endured but my ears are now about half an inch farther forward than is normal.

I found myself attracted more and more to the pier end of the beach, where the boats were moored. This now has a concrete slipway and a brass plate reading 'Edward Heath Slipped Here' but in those days there was just a lot of seaweed and a few moored dinghies gently banging into each other. What with the seaweed and the toffee papers and the Choc-Ice wrappers it was not so much messing about in boats as boating about in mess.

Very soon the Dinghy Set had accepted me as a sort of mascot and I spent all my time with them. Sometimes one of them would take me out for a sail and let me lower the centre-board and do a bit of bailing, and I would run all the way home, ten feet tall, freezing cold, with a soaking wet bottom.

They were all very much older than me. My particular hero was the group's acknowledged leader, Guy Beauchamp, a middle-aged man of about twenty-two. Most of the others shared a boat between them but Guy had his own, which he worked on all day, touching up varnish and tightening the stays. I spoke very little in those days. Not because I was timid but because I usually had a chunk of Uncle William's toffee in my mouth and as the toffee was broken off a block with a toffee-hammer and the pieces were usually large, pointed triangles which almost pierced the cheeks, any attempt at speech usually resulted in the listener being drenched with a fine spray of Banana-Flavour juice. But Guy spoke even less than I did. His conversation seemed to be entirely restricted to laconic, one-word instructions; ‘Anchor’, he would say. And perhaps an hour later, ‘Oar’. He had fair hair, a cleft in his chin, and he wore khaki shorts which came just below the knee and a roll-neck sweater apparently knitted from spaghetti. He pottered about in the water all day getting his feet wet and never caught cold. A tremendously impressive chap.

His girl friend was Carmen Rowbottom, the ironmonger's daughter, although Mr Rowbottom called it ‘Row-both-am’ because he had married the gas manager's daughter and was a sidesman. I could never see much to Carmen at the time. She was quite elderly, pushing twenty, and wasn't very interesting to look at, having rather a lot of loose hair, like a carthorse's ankle, and huge bumps above her waist which got in the way when she rowed. But Guy was very keen on her, taking her for long, silent sails.

At the other end of the scale was Charlie Gordon who worked as a reporter on the *East Kent Messenger*. He was known as ‘Toothy’ because he hadn't got many, due to a cricket-ball. Toothy was small, bow-legged and ugly. He spent most of the time sitting on the edge of the pier, not helping, making rather funny comments.

Then it happened. There had been a week of bad weather and none of us had been on the beach. I was sitting on the pier wondering when

46

the rain would ease up when I found Carmen standing there, eyes sparkling.

"I'm married!" she said.

For a while I couldn't speak. I'd swallowed my lump of toffee. When the pain in my chest had diminished I lifted one earpiece of my bathing hat so as not to miss a word and wished her and Guy a lifetime of bliss.

"Not Guy," she said. "Toothy. I'm Mrs Gordon!"

"But . . ." I said, which wasn't much help but it was all I could think of to say in the stress of the moment.

"Be a sweet and tell Guy for me, will you? It'll be easier coming from you." And with a wifely peck on my cheek she was gone.

I found Guy in the sail-locker, darning a sail.

"Er, Guy, er," I said. "Er, Carmen's married. Asked me to tell you. Married Toothy. She's Mrs Gordon."

Guy stared at me with his unblinking, mariner's gaze.

"They're married," I repeated. "Married. Wed. Mr and Mrs Gordon."

Still no response.

"Miss Rowbotham has joined Mr Gordon in Holy Matrimony . . ."

As I ploughed on a horrifying truth dawned upon me. The splendid Guy, my idol, was as thick as a post. As dim as a nun's nightlight.

"Your ex-girl-friend and the man with few teeth are as one . . ."

But nothing was registering. As I sweated on, trying to get the message home to him, the scales dropping from my eyes like autumn leaves in a gale, I realised that My Hero was a man of few words because he only knew a few. In fact, apart from a few everyday phrases like 'Pass the marmalade', and 'Does this train stop at Faversham?' his entire vocabulary was nautical.

And so I translated my message into the language he knew.

"Mr Gordon and Miss Rowbotham," I said, "have sailed together into the harbour of matrimony. And are moored together for life."

Immediately he understood. His figure sagged. He seemed to be trying to say something.

I stood with him, but my words of comfort were of no use.

At dawn the following morning a longshoreman, out early to dig bait and nick things from the bathing huts, found Guy as I had left him; staring into space and muttering over and over again the harsh truth which he had, somehow, to accept:

"Carmen . . . Toothy Gordon . . . Moored!"

The game is not worth the candle

Proverb

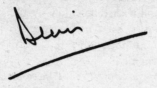

CONTINUING our series, Cameos Of The Great Composers, the spotlight falls today on George Frederick Handel, the man who cleffed such great musicals as *Acis and Galatea*, both of which must be familiar to all lovers of the semi-classics.

Born in Germany, Handel acquired, according to the *Oxford Dictionary of Music*, 'a great reputation as a keyboard performer', a statement which we can only hope means he played the piano. After a spell as Kapellmeister to the Elector of Hanover, a dying craft nowadays, he came to England and took up residence just outside Edgeware in 1710. At least we believe that to have been his room-number but many pages of the parish-records were torn out in the Great Plague, there being no cleaning-tissues in those days.

However, the composer was immediately made welcome by the Edgeware gentry, for even in those days Handel was a name which opens all doors. As a young bachelor with several concerti grossi under his belt, to say nothing of his Harmonious Blacksmith, he was especially courted by parents of unmarried daughters and it was in this connection that he was accosted one day by Sir Tenleigh Knott.

Sir Tenleigh, a member of the old nobility, was the sixth son of the seventh Earl – or it may have been the seventh son of the sixth Earl, it was very difficult to tell with all those winding staircases – and he possessed an unmarried daughter, Arabella. She was a vivacious girl, not pretty by any accepted standards, if anything ugly by any accepted standards, but she could speak Latin and foot a quadrille and sometimes the two simultaneously if the tempo was right. So it was of her that Sir Tenleigh bethought himself when he espied Handel by the Long

Meadow, for in those days Edgeware was all fields even the agricultural land.

"Ah," said Sir Tenleigh, greeting him boisterously, "George Frederick Handel, isn't it?"

"Isn't it what?" said Handel, betraying his Teutonic meticulousness.

"Isn't it a shame that a nice young fellow like you should still be unmarried," said Sir Tenleigh, who never believed in shilly-shallying. "It's unnatural, that's what it is. I'll wager that since you arrived in this country, the only thing you've taken out is your naturalisation papers."

The remark contained enough truth to give Handel pause. Only too well did he know the torments of the flesh, having been up all the previous night with indigestion, a consequence of researching 'Alexander's Feast'. A wife who might be as adept at cooking as she was fair and slim of limb was a prospect which appealed to him strongly. So, "You have maybe somebody in mind?" he asked.

"My daughter Arabella," came the elder man's prompt reply. "An extremely vivacious girl. Gay, jolly, you might even say sporty."

"What does she look like?"

It was the age of 'arranged' marriages, as distinct from today's 'untidy' ones, so it was no unusual thing for two young people to be wed without ever having seen each other before the ceremony. Nevertheless, "What does she look like?," Handel asked.

"Foots a quadrille while speaking perfect Latin," said old Sir Tenleigh. "You have made a wise choice."

"What does she look like?"

"How's the *Messiah* going? Finished the Honolulu Chorus yet?"

"What does she look like?"

"Tell you what I'm prepared to do," Sir Tenleigh said. "I am willing to settle an estate on her." The truth was, Arabella had a shape it was perfectly possible to settle an estate on. Her main drawback had always been her resemblance to an early Georgian road-block but it was not a factor Sir Tenleigh felt like discussing.

"What does she look like?" enquired Handel again.

"You have made an old man very happy," said Sir Tenleigh, shaking his hand warmly. "Welcome to the Knott family."

"What does she look like?" Handel called after his departing figure, receiving in reply a cheery wave.

It was a troubled George Frederick who sat that night weighing up half a pound of toccatas. Somewhere deep within him he felt the vague unease that sometimes besets a man when he realises he's marrying a woman he's never laid eyes on. On impulse, he called in his man-servant, a devoted local rustic named Walter, to whom the composer later dedicated his chart-topping *Handel's Walter Music*. "I want you should run an errand for me," Handel said tossing him a florin, and we must remember that in those days a florin was worth – what? Two shillings, at least. "Go take a look at Miss Arabella Knott."

"'Ow will oi know 'er?" enquired Walter.

"She'll be the one footing a quadrille in Latin, very gay with it."

"What do 'ee want to know about 'er?" asked the rustic.

"What does she look like?"

When Walter returned, Handel could hardly wait to get the details, having by this time got himself worked up into a right state. "Tell me," he demanded eagerly, "Was she tall and fair, the vivacious Arabella? Was she a delicate wand of beauty? Was she straight as a yew-tree, slim as far-off violins?"

The rustic, in his slow way, sighed. What was the gentlest way he could break the news of Arabella's dimensions to this quivering Hun? Perhaps the only course was to be blunt. "Oi be sorry," he replied –

"The gay Miss Knott were thick, Handel."

Frank

THERE has been a fatality in the village. The taped
music in the Saloon Bar of the 'Red Lion' was switched off for twenty-
four hours as a mark of respect, Mrs Dean removed the prop from her
clothes-line and flew her washing at half-mast, Mrs Macnamara wore
a black band on her sleeve but as her coat was also black nobody
noticed, and the village schoolchildren, on a nature ramble, punched
each other in a muted fashion, as though their hearts weren't in it.

Philomel, the donkey, has passed away, and the opening ceremony of
the Thorpe Grand Autumn Fair Admission Free All Proceeds to
Village Charities will never be the same. Never again will Mr Johns,
the chairman, say "Ladies and gentleman, it gives me great pleasure to
declare this year's Thorpe Grand Autumn Fair open . . ." only to be
interrupted by a window-rattling bray and the entrance of Philomel.
She would pause in front of the platform, paw the ground twice, roll
an eye, and then sink onto her front elbows and waggle her tail at Mr
Johns. One year she pawed the floor three times and forgot to roll her
eye; several children burst into tears and there was a very stiff letter
indeed in the following Thursday's local paper. Philomel's annual
appearance had to be exactly the same each year. Young men would
emigrate from Thorpe to Australia, marry, and return to Thorpe
confident that their offspring would witness exactly the same ceremony
that they had witnessed as ladlings. Philomel represented tradition, and
continuity.

Mr Johns' eye was moist at the Parish Council meeting last night. "It
wouldn't be a Thorpe Grand Autumn Fair without Philomel, me
dears," he said. He was right, too.

It wasn't really much of a Grand Fair *with* Philomel. Thorpe Village

Hall is on the small side and only accommodates a few stalls. First came the games. There was the popular bucket-of-water-with-a-sixpence-in-the-bottom; the idea being to drop pennies into the water in the wistful hope that one would cover the sixpence and win a small prize. The trouble with that game was that since inflation and decimalisation one had to drop a 2p piece and attempt to cover a 10p piece, which is larger than a 2p piece.

Next came a game of rolling rubber balls down an inclined plane in an attempt to get them into holes. Unhappily the board had warped over the years and however you rolled the balls they all ended up in the bottom left-hand corner.

The most popular item came next; a stiff, wriggly wire along which you were supposed to pass a brass curtain-ring. The thing was wired up so that if your hand trembled a bell rang. The wires were still there but the old-fashioned battery had become obsolete fifteen years ago so the bell did not ring and everybody won a prize.

Then there was the cake stall. The home-made cakes were so popular that they were all bought by the other stall-holders before the Fair opened.

And finally there was the ever-popular Jumble stall. For the last twenty years this has consisted of a slightly rusty golf-club with the string unwinding from the handle, the sole survivor of a pair of book-ends, a pottery biscuit barrel with the knob missing from the lid and the brass showing through the chromium, a glass 'snow-storm' paper-weight with the Eiffel Tower inside which you turned upside down and nothing happened, a pianola roll of 'Marche Militaire', and four books: *Hiawatha, Rendered into Latin*, F. W. Newman, 1862; *Our Debt and Duty to the Soil, The Poetry and Philosophy of Sewage Utilisation*, E. D. Girdlestone, 1878; *Little Elsie's Book of Bible Animals*, 1878; and *Hindustani Self-Taught by the Natural Method*, E. Marlborough, 1908.

When I first came to the village I did not understand how these fêtes and fairs worked. I bought the biscuit barrel and kept it for tobacco. I was quietly corrected by the energetic lady who collected all the jumble for the various functions, Mrs Rumbold.

"If you don't mind me pointing out," she said, "these items are for buying and handing back, not for keeping. What you do is give the biscuit barrel back to me and it comes up at the Church Christmas Bazaar. I then collect it for the Scouts Hut Fund Jamboree. After that it goes to the Young Wives' Bring-and-Buy, the Annual Village Fête, the Darby and Joan White Elephant Night, the Thorpe Dramatic

Society Bargain Sale, and it then ends up again at the Thorpe Grand Autumn Fair. It brings in sixpence a time. If you hang on to it, Mr Muir, you are depriving village charities of three shillings and sixpence per annum."

My cheek mantling, I handed the biscuit barrel to Mrs Rumbold to be put back into circulation.

So you see the Grand Autumn Fair could hardly be described as a riveting, compulsive, not-to-be-missed-at-any-cost event. Except for Philomel.

"How did she . . . ?" I asked Mr Johns.

"Internal trouble." he said, quietly. "Sam is heartbroken."

Sam Thornton, the ancient old jobbing gardener, was not only Philomel's owner, he was also her front legs. Her back legs were occupied by Sam's brother Ron. Twenty years ago Ron had been lifting some leeks when his back clicked and he found that he had locked at right angles. He soon got used to walking about with his back at ninety degrees to his legs and Sam, being community minded, decided to make use of Ron's affliction for the good of charity and make him the back half of a pantomime donkey. Sam got the lady on the green who does bespoke loose covers for sofas to make the body out of canvas, Mr Hyde, the Egham saddler, made leather hooves and a papier-mâché head – and Philomel was born. Sam loved his moment of glory. Every first of September he would rub his hands and say, "Come on Ron, time to get the old moke working!" And they would practise for weeks.

"Last week," said Mr Johns. "Ron accidentally backed into a pitch-fork and straightened up for the first time in twenty years. Trouble was, though, he locked upright. Couldn't bend an inch. Sam had to find somebody else to work the back half. Do you know his great-nephew Fred?"

"City lad from Staines?" I said. "Bit thick? Keeps putting his skid-lid on back to front and riding into walls?"

"That's him. Well, Sam has been training him up to be the back legs. Last night Sam was giving him an extra hour's waggling practice when the lad suddenly went quiet. The next thing Sam knew was a terrible pain, a searing agony in his behind. He couldn't help leaping forward. The old, half-perished canvas ripped, and poor old Philomel was torn in half."

"But why the pain? What . . . ?"

"Fred had lit up a cigarette. The old boy couldn't bear to cope with

Philomel's remains so I took her to the road-sweeper, who was cleaning the drain by the bus-stop, and . . . I had her put down."

To break the long silence I said, "Well, I suppose we go ahead anyway with getting the jumble together and getting the cakes baked. . . ?"

"No," said Mr Johns. And he put into words what we, and the whole village, knew to be a sad but real truth:

"There is no Fair without Sam's moke."

"MR NORDEN," said this temporary shorthand-typist. "One more criticism about my spelling and I shall resign. You hear me? R-E-Z-Y-N, resign!"

Once again I silently maligned Brenda's husband. Brenda is my real secretary, the permanent one. A dear sweet girl, she's been with me for fifteen years, never a word of complaint, always unerringly efficient. Then, last year, she had the unmitigated gall to go and get married. And it was while she was away on her honeymoon – three whole days if you don't mind! – that I was forced to acquaint myself with that phenomenon of modern office life, the temporary secretary. Or, as they advertise themselves, 'Temps'.

For those of you who may be still unfamiliar with this consciousness-lowering group, let me explain their significance. You know how God dictated the Ten Commandments to Moses? Well if, instead of Moses, he had dictated them to a Temp – we would now all be working on only Four Commandments. Temps come in every size and shape but there are three characteristics shared by all of them: the first is a total unfamiliarity with the language the British use when communicating with each other, the second is the most tenuous acquaintanceship with the skills of shorthand and typing, the third is extremely little between the ear-rings.

I well remember the first one who came in to give a helping hand, at a hire-charge of 75p per hour per finger. Brenda was going off on another pleasure jaunt, some frivolity connected with a burst appendix, so I phoned the Agency to send over a temporary typist. What turned up was a lanky creature who, with her platform shoes and metal hair rollers, appeared to be about seven foot tall. Looking for all the world like a sexy radar-mast, she marched straight over to the typewriter, sat down and hit some keys. "Oh, look," she said. "It makes little letters."

When the next one arrived, I was somewhat cagier. "Before you start," I said, "could you tell me your speeds?"

"Well, I'm afraid I only do thirty words a minute," she said.

"Is that shorthand or typing?"

"No," she said, "reading."

To list all the agonies I have endured would be as boring for you as they were painful to me. On one occasion I went into Brenda's office to see how a short fat Temp was getting on with typing one of my letters, because when I'd dictated it to her she'd interrupted to ask how to spell comma. I found her sitting at the desk using two typewriters simultaneously; one with the left hand, the other with the right hand. Noticing my stupefaction, she gave a nervous smile. "I'm sorry," she said, "I couldn't find any carbon paper."

"How are you on the switchboard?" I asked one who'd pitched up looking like an explosion in a remnants factory. "Dunno," she replied. "I never done it on there." I remember the girl who arrived four hours late, having got out of the lift one floor down and spent the whole morning working for the wrong firm; the one who tried to look up telephone numbers in the *Oxford Dictionary*; the one who insisted on having a manual typewriter but an electric eraser. I had one girl who took snuff and another whose only previous commercial experience had been as a commère in a Dolphinarium.

I don't know what qualifications the Agencies require from a girl before they send her out. My private belief is that they show each applicant a washing-machine, a refrigerator and a typewriter. If she can identify the typewriter, she's on the books. What I know for certain is that ever since Brenda's perfidy forced me into availing myself of these creatures, I am become but a Xerox of my former self. Last week I asked one of them if she would fetch me a book of synonyms. "Oh, I love his books," she said. "Specially the Maigrets."

The breaking-point came this morning. A new Temp had arrived – the usual type, dolled up to the nines and trailing glories of cloudiness. After I had dictated my first letter to her, I said cautiously, "Do you think you could read it to me back, please?"

"Beg pardon?"

"Please read it to me back."

You won't believe this. That girl got up and started to *walk round behind me*. . . .

That's when I cried 'enough'. "No more temporary secretaries until further notice!" I screamed down the phone to the Agency.

It was only when the twitching ceased that it occurred to me that there might have been a more succinct way of putting the request. Musically. The way Peter Dawson used to sing it –

"Hold Further Temps!"

'Maybe It's Because I'm A Londoner'

Hubert Gregg
Title of Song

Frank

I'M retired now, of course. I retired about, oooh, no it was before that. I retired twice, as a matter of fact. For many years I worked for the General Post Office. I was employed at the Charing Cross Road, London, branch to stand behind a window and say, "I'm sorry but this window is closed, try the next one up". But when I retired from that my sister made me take another job for a week and retire again, because she didn't fancy having a brother who was a retired postal worker, in however responsible a position. That is the sister who was on the stage but is now in Dorking. She married, you know. Quite a few times. If my memory does not play me false, she is now married, or was at the time of her last Christmas card, to a gentleman who processes the films for a photographer attached to a local estate agency. She always refers to him as 'my husband the Property Developer'. So to please her I took a job at a garage for a week, coiling up the air-line used for inflating tyres, and then retired again. She always refers to me as 'my brother the retired Air-Line Executive'.

I am quite happy in my little room, not a stone's throw from Notting Hill. It is what is called a Bed-Sit. That is to say, if you want to sit you have to sit on the bed. I've lived in this same room for, it must be, oooh, or was it the year that, um. . . .

Until I found my little friend, my pet, I became rather lonely. I had my music, of course. I hum a great deal when I am on my own, sometimes accompanying myself on an old bongo drum which the previous tenant used for storing dried melon seeds. It is, I suppose, a humdrum existence, but there we are.

Ah. I was telling you of my pet. Well, I became lonely when I found

58

it increasingly difficult to move about either swiftly or for any length of time. I am on the ninth floor and I soon found that although I could get down the stairs without difficulty I only had enough energy left to get back up again, with none to spare for going out. I had a friend, a Miss Winstanley, who lived in the basement. She was for many years Miss-On-Cash in a Mayfair butcher's shop until she retired some, oooh, it must now, let me see. . . . Well, we came to an arrangement whereby we met halfway down, or in her case halfway up, the stairs. There we would chat, d'you see, of the weather and similar topics, and we would return to our own rooms in fair condition, having divided the expenditure of energy between us.

But after a year or so we both began to feel less capable of tackling the stairs. It was all right when we each managed three flights, we could lean over the banisters and shout to each other. However, we soon could only manage two flights each and as neither of us could see or hear the other, with five flights of stairs in between, there seemed little point in continuing the arrangement.

That was when I began to feel lonely. Unhappily dogs and cats were strictly forbidden in the house. Rather surprising, really, because the landlord, Mr Carew-Entwistle-Carew, is clearly a dog-lover; he always arrives to collect the rent with two Doberman pinschers.

Then one day the problem was solved for me. I did not find myself a pet; a pet found me.

It was a bee. A handsome, brown bee. He was so plump and had such a rich fur coat that I christened him Diaghilev. I presume he must have fallen from a hive that was being transported through London on the back of a lorry because he was obviously lost and quite grateful to have somewhere to rest his head. I made him a little nest in the bongo drum and he took to staying with me all night and most of the day, buzzing off occasionally when he felt like it. He was free to come and go as he pleased; if the window was shut he could always fly out through the hole in the ceiling where the slate blew off in 1961, or through the aperture in the wall where I rather imagine a wash-basin used to be.

Diaghilev and I got along splendidly for some weeks but then he began to lose weight. As the days sped past he became thinner and thinner until he no longer looked like a ballet impresario but more like the last half-inch of a used pipe-cleaner. I was in despair, as you might well imagine. And then I realised the problem was simply food. Bees eat nectar, and Diaghilev must have buzzed himself half silly trying to find nectar in Notting Hill.

I sprang, at my own pace, into action. I coerced my nice Health Visitor to bring me up a bucket of soil and a selection of honeysuckle plants. These I put into an old, oblong wooden box, which I had used for many years to hold my boot-cleaning things. This I fixed on my, albeit crumbling, window-ledge. I watered the plants with great care, and they flourished.

Oh, the joy of watching Diaghilev restore himself to health! I could not see the expression on his little face as he dipped, soared, buzzed, and then settled over the honeysuckle flowers – my eyes are not what they were – but I am sure that he wore a happy look. In a few days he filled out and became his old, sleek self again.

My cup of happiness became full a week later. He found himself a girl friend, a smaller, even sleeker bee, whom he brought home to show off his window box. And quite suddenly one morning I noticed that Diaghilev was buzzing a different buzz, a high-pitched, interrupted buzz. He was engaged!

Every now and then somebody comes on the wireless and talks about bee-keeping, and they always say that you can't keep bees in a city, that to keep bees you need to own land so that they can have acres of fields and flowers to feed on. I just smile, and look at fat, happy Diaghilev buzzing round my window-box, and I hum a little hum to myself. I hum –

'My bee eats because I'm a landowner!'

A rose is a rose is a rose

Gertrude Stein
'*Sacred Emily*'

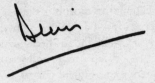

HOW strange! How really very strange! Do you know, that's the second time today I've come across that line. Isn't that a coincidence? No, really, sometimes I go for weeks without encountering 'a rose is a rose is a rose' but today – twice! Small world. This very morning I saw it written down on a note-pad at my psychiatrist's.

Did I tell you I've got this new psychiatrist now? Well, I never really had the confidence in that other fellow. I mean how much confidence can you have in a man who tries to cure a somatic anxiety-depressive psychosis with an ointment? Oh yes, very distinguished-looking, I admit, but that day I came in and heard him saying into the telephone, "Mummy, you'll just have to face up to it, I'm moving into my own flat" – well, that was it. "I'm sorry," I said, "but I must ask you for my symptoms back."

This new man now, what a difference! Don't go asking me whether he's the Jungian school or the Adlerian school because I can't tell you, all I know is it's the one that costs seven guineas a visit, but where the confidence-inspiring is concerned – chalk and cheese. And it's more than just the fact of no longer having to go through a barber's shop to get to him, it's his methods.

Dreams, you see. That's his thing. "I do tend to go a bundle on dreams," he told me when I signed on with him. So what I have to do now is, I have to keep some paper on the bedside-table and whenever I have a dream, get down a description of it the moment I wake up. Mind you, she leads off a bit about it, the Madam, because of the noise of the typewriter in the middle of the night. But the psychiatrist says take no mind of that, all women are troublemakers, he says, the Greeks had the right idea. Then twice a week I go along to him, lie down on his couch, a rexine one it is and he says the small change that slips down the sides, that's where the real money in psychiatry lies, and after I've read out my dreams to him he interprets them.

Which I must say is more than I could ever do. Just rubbish most of them seem to me, not to mention downright suggestive sometimes. Take the one I was telling him about this morning, the one where I was in a Cowboys and Indians scene. Now I agree that's one I do dream a lot but I've always put it down to childhood, because what with all those Randolph Scott pictures us kids used to go and see up the Regal, we were always playing Cowboys and Indians games. Not that I was ever allowed to be a Cowboy or an Indian in those games, that was always for the stronger boys. Me being so delicate, and like better dressed, I always used to be the lady having a baby in the end waggon.

But it stays in your unconscious, doesn't it, there's no denying it, so in this dream I was telling the psychiatrist about, I was in a waggon-train going along the prairie when suddenly thump-thump-thump, a storm of arrows on the roof. Comanches!

Up gallops the Waggon-master, and I remember something else now, should have told the psychiatrist this, in our games the Waggon-master was always the strongest fighter in the gang, so up gallops Alice, with arrows sticking out all over her, and she shouts, "Get the waggons in a circle."

Now you know how it is with dreams. Immediately she said the words "in a circle" there I was travelling on the Inner Circle. If you don't know what the Inner Circle is, it's part of the London Under-ground, a transport system which enables you to travel from say Liverpool Street to Blackfriars very much quicker than if you tried to get there crawling on your hands and knees. Anyway, there I was on the Inner Circle and I was stark naked.

"Symbolic," the psychiatrist said when I said that to him.

"All right," I said, "I was symbolic naked." Come to think of it, it's funny really how many of my dreams I do seem to wind up stark symbolic naked. When I'm not having a baby that is. But, as I say, I was travelling naked on the Inner Circle and while I was trying to remember where I could have put my ticket, suddenly the train stops at a station, I look out the window from idle curiosity and what do I see? It's Harrow.

And now it happens again. The moment I see the word 'Harrow', just as suddenly as last time – I'm the Headmaster of Harrow School. May I go blind, the Headmaster of Harrow School. Mortarboard, cane and full sidewhiskers. Otherwise stark naked, of course. And there, bending over in front of me, in a school cap and short trousers, is the psychiatrist. "Stop blubbing, boy," I hear myself saying, "you're down for six of the best."

Now when I got to this bit, the old psychiatrist perked up no end. He stopped shaving, put his electric razor down and came and sat down right there on the couch with me. "And did you cane me?" he says, nibbling his lip. "Talk slower."

Well, as it happens, I didn't cane him. Because, in the dream, just as I raise the cane, I notice he's got something knobbly tucked down the back of his trousers, so I stop. "Whatever you've got down there, boy," I say to him, "fetch it out." So he reaches behind into the seat of his trousers and know what he pulls out? A bust of Cicero. Now how I recognise it's a bust of Cicero is because he's got one himself in his surgery, the psychiatrist, and he showed me it one day. He's got lots of Greek statues round his walls come to think of it, though they're mainly of young fellows carrying wine-cups.

Anyway, in the dream, after he's pulled out the bust of Cicero, I say to him, "Sure there's nothing else down there, lad?" and he sobs "Yes, sir." And from the same place he pulls out another bust of Cicero. Then another one, then another one.

And from then on, the sort of nightmare-thing sets in, because he keeps on pulling them out. One bust of Cicero after another, thirty of them, forty of them. And just when the whole room is getting waist-deep in busts of Cicero – I wake up.

Now, I ask you, what would you have made of a dream like that? Going from a Comanche Indian Raid, to Harrow Station on the Inner Circle, to God knows how many busts of Cicero – wouldn't you say just a lot of old nonsense? No logic in it all?

Me too. But that's why I've got the confidence in this new man. With his college-training, what he deduced right away was that I was revolting. And what was I revolting against? Some old bird called Gertrude Stein. Because, showing me the three little notes he'd made on his note-pad, he said what they represented was my unconscious rejection of Gertrude Stein.

What he'd written, you see, was –

"Arrows . . . sees Harrow . . . Ciceros."

Allons, enfants de la patrie!

Rouget de Lisle
'*La Marseillaise*'

Frank

I had this nasty experience with a pair of trousers. For years I bought my trousers from the same shop, a dimly lit, mahogany-panelled oasis of calm in an alley off Bond Street. Mr Herring, who was about a hundred and four, would creep forward, fingering the tape measure round his neck, and ask my pleasure. Having selected a likely pair of trousers I would be waved into the Changing Cabinet to try them on. The Changing Cabinet was about the size of an average hotel bedroom and it always contained Mr Herring's partner, Mr Butterfield, furtively eating egg sandwiches. Mr Butterfield, who was about a hundred and six, would mumble apologies and back out, shedding crumbs, and I would examine myself in a spotted pier-glass while Mr Herring fussed round me ensuring that the trousers fitted snugly under the arm-pits and that there was plenty of room in the seat for sitting.

When I went back there a few months ago the shop had gone. In its place was a shop selling Japanese cameras and coloured slides of the Changing of the Guard, so I had, perforce, to find another seller of trousers. It's all changed, hasn't it? Whereas I once dealt with Herring, Butterfield and Nephew (Estd. 1901), I found myself entering a shop called the Kensington Panty Boo-Teak.

And there was no Changing Cabinet. When it came to trying on the trousers I was shown a row of booths up against the wall. These had no door, as such, just a pair of extremely inadequate cowboy saloon swing doors, about eighteen inches deep, hung half-way up.

I don't know what the height of the normal trouser tryer-onner is but I don't think that it is six feet six inches, which is what I am. The vulnerable area was in grave danger; indeed, had I been wearing unduly thick socks I would probably have been arrested. But worse was to follow. It was impossible, I found, to remove one pair of trousers and encase the legs in a trendy new pair whilst standing bolt upright. A certain amount of knee-bending was unavoidable. It was while I was doubled over in a kind of foetal crouch trying to get my feet into the new trousers that I found myself gazing into the eyes of a lady sitting on a couch opposite. The full horror then dawned. Not only was any kind of privacy impossible but it was a mixed establishment open to both sexes. I shouted for an assistant, because the trousers, by an error of manufacture, appeared to have the zip at the back, to be faced by a ravishing Deb-of-the-Year who promptly burst into squeals of laughter and shrieked to the whole shop that I'd put my trousers on back to front.

I staggered out of the booth feeling very wobbly indeed. All I wanted was a sit-down for a few minutes. I sagged into a seat and closed my eyes. Almost immediately I heard a male voice say, "You look a bit ribby, squire. Permit me to do the laying on of the hands."

I opened my eyes to see an odd figure looming over me. He was wearing a wide, black sombrero, and a cloak of some dark material, underneath which was a bus conductor's uniform.

"Hold still, guv," he said. He put his fingers on my head, kneaded the scalp a bit, and hummed the opening bars of 'La Marseillaise'. "Ta-tum, ti-tum, tum, ta, ti, TA, ti-tum . . . Feeling better now?"

"No," I said. "Exactly as before."

"Blast!" he said. "It's no go, I'm afraid. Oh, well, it was worth trying."

He joined me on the seat and handed me a card. It read 'Alonzo Rathbone. Layer-On Of Hands. Cures While-U-Wait.'

"But," I said, "you're a bus conductor."

"Professionally I conduct buses, that is true." he said. "But by vocation, I am a Healer."

"Of people?"

"Well, no. That's the problem. So far, only plants. I was hoping for a breakthrough with you, but alas, it was not meant. My Granny's glad."

"What about?"

"No, no", he said. "Her glad. Her gladioli. That's how I discovered I had this gift. The gladioli were wilting and I was touching them, fondling them, and I began to hum the opening bars of the Marseillaise, and suddenly my finger-tips went all trembly and I could feel a kind of energy leaving me and entering into the glad. Next day the glad was so sprightly that Gran entered it in the Stoke Newington Darby and Joan flower show and won a linen tea-towel with a recipe for bouillabaisse printed on it. Sorry I couldn't help you, guv, but if you ever have trouble with wilting plants, fruit trees, leguminous veg, just get in touch with me. Remember the name, Alonzo Rathbone." And with a swing of his cloak he strode off to the bus depot.

I forgot all about Alonzo until a few days ago. I don't know about you but we have had a disastrous year in the garden. The front gate got Dutch Elm disease; the white paint turned yellow and the top bar crumbled away. The new rose bed was too near the oil central heating chimney and all the roses went down with flue. The lawn stopped growing, went brown, and still had a new mown look after seven weeks; a classic case of newmownia. But worst of all our Comice peartree had a nervous breakdown.

"Look at it!" said my wife, her face twisted with grief. "Our oldest tree! Our delight! And now – brown leaves, bark flaking away. And look at the pears! They look more like spotty nutmegs!"

It certainly looked a goner.

"My favourite tree in the whole garden. The whole world," said my wife, plying the hanky. "Doomed. Nobody can save it now!"

"Alonzo!" I yelled, without warning.

"What?"

"There is just a chance in a million that I know a man who could restore it to health. With his 'fluence. He touches them up!"

I hurtled upstairs and found the trousers I had bought at the Boo-Teak. I had never worn them because when I got them home they seemed to have been designed for a seventeen year old, colour-blind neuter, but inside the hip pocket was the card I was looking for, reading 'Alonzo Rathbone. Layer-On Of Hands. Cures While-U-Wait'. But – oh, misery – no address.

But you never know your luck. Perhaps bus conductors read books like this to while away the time between rush hours. If so I have a message for a Mr Rathbone. More than a message, really, a plea to make two middle-aged fruit fanciers happy:

"Alonzo, fondle our pear-tree!"

Sweet are the uses of adversity

William Shakespeare
'*As You Like It*'

Denis

IN a previous book of 'My Word!' stories (*A finger on the pulse of our time. . . F. Muir*), I made mention of Mrs Thora Tidmarsh, our local High Priestess where cultural matters are concerned. Mrs Tidmarsh is a strapping clear-eyed lady, well-built without being the slightest bit sexy, like a Junior Minister's wife, and if Concorde had been able to develop the same amount of thrust it would now be plying the Atlantic. As is often the way with such ladies, her husband Arthur, although an extremely good credit-risk, is so totally devoid of personality he gives the impression he'd come out black and white even on colour TV. At the soirées which established his wife's ascendancy as local arbiter on all questions artistic, her Sunday Afternoon Musical Teas, he was little more than a plate-passer.

Those Sunday afternoons were occasions of absolutely teeth-aching refinement. They took place in her lovely dining-room, a muted mixture of all the more expensive greens and browns but furnished with so many marble-top tables it was like eating in an indoor cemetery. While you munched hopelessly at unidentifiable squares of thin bread, Mrs Tidmarsh played – and thoroughly explained – records of what is called 'atonal' music. It is called that, I most sincerely hope, because somebody, sometime, is going to have to atone for it. Of the whole experience, what I remember most clearly is that peculiar ache in the neck one only gets from too much nodding appreciatively.

However, because the presence of every person invited was unfailingly reported in the local press, Mrs Tidmarsh's Musical Teas became a sort of social Access Card. If the Manager of the Supermarket had noticed your name among the list of those attending, his man at the check-out could be persuaded to help hump your shopping out to the car. For that reason no-one ever turned down an invite and Mrs Tidmarsh reigned unchallenged as cultural champ of N.W.11.

Unchallenged, that is, until the arrival in the neighbourhood of Alf and Rowena Hughes. The first hint that these two might qualify as contenders for the title came from the milkman, our quartier's acknowledged William Hickey. "Hey," he said, "know them new people who've taken Number Seventy-Four? They're installing one of them libidos in their bathroom."

It was – insofar as such an item can be so designated – a straw in the wind. Our suspicions that the Hugheses might prove persons of social consequence were strengthened when the local paper printed a story that Rowena intended to stage a Women's Liberation protest demonstration at the next Hampstead Heath Bank Holiday Fair. "I intend to lead a march," she was reported as saying, "demanding the abolition of Halfway For Ladies at the coconut-shy."

The actual gauntlet was thrown down in the form of a startling handwritten invitation stuffed into all our letter-boxes. Startling, I mean, by Tidmarsh literary standards. "Hi, new neighbours!" it read, in day-glo colours, "It's getting-to-know-ya time! Why not mosey up the trail to the Hughes ranch 4 pm this Sunday? Strong drink, light nosh and Poetry Reading!"

Poetry Reading! Well, I can tell you, the Washeteria that Saturday was a veritable buzz of indecision and in the Supermarket there was a five-cart pile-up. Was Sunday to be the Hugheses or the Tidmarshes? On the credit side, the milkman's last broadcast had stated that the Hughes's drawing room contained an ozone-spraying humidifier and inflatable Queen Anne chairs. On the debit side, might not the exchange of explained-music for spoken-poetry turn out to be a frying-pan and fire situation?

"Depends what kind of poetry it is," said the man from Number Sixteen, who runs a boutique called Mad Togs For Englishmen. "Like, T. S. Eliot like, he's quite catchy. My Mum had a record of him doing 'I used To Sigh For The Silvery Moon', you could get the hang of it practically first go off."

"Could we perhaps ring and *ask* them what kind of poetry?" offered Mr Twenty-Eight, who manufactures pregnant window-dummies for Mothercare. It was a bright suggestion so he was deputed to go and make the phone call.

He came back wearing a rather dazed expression. "Guess what?" he said. "The Golden Treasury of Erotic Verse!"

So that's how Thora Tidmarsh's supremacy was broken, that's how a musical experience was exchanged for a literary experience, that's how wife-swapping got started in Hampstead Garden Suburb.

What often runs through my mind, though, is the phrase that Thora must have used to Arthur on the following Monday morning – after the milkman had arrived to tell her exactly *why* her Sunday afternoon audience had deserted her.

"Sweetheart," she must have said –

"Sweetheart, the Hugheses offer verse at tea."

If at first you don't succeed, try, try again

William Edward Hickson
'Try and Try Again'

Frank

"I T is time," said my wife, "that you gave the puppy a bath."

A simple, friendly, wifely statement, spoken in a gentle, well-modulated tone, and yet my innards twisted into a knot. What was an undeniable truth was that Lady Ottoline Morrell – for that was our Afghan hound puppy's name – was, at the age of fifteen months, a bit old to be called a puppy, and was very long overdue for her first bath. As the condition of our house bore witness.

To begin with, the phrase 'giving the puppy a bath' conjures up a picture of gently dunking a scrap of fur in a pudding-basin of warm suds. It inadequately describes wrestling desperately with four and a half stone of powerfully-sinewed, wilful, furious doormat. I couldn't get her anywhere near the pudding-basin.

It might well be that high up in the hills of Afghanistan above Kabul a simple old shepherd had only to whistle once through blackened teeth for his obedient hound to round up a herd of alpaca, or cashmere goats, or whatever they rear up there to make those smelly coats out of, before leaping unbidden into a hot bath. But our puppy's mother came from Chelmsford, and the native skills seem to have been bred out of the strain in the soft life of the Home Counties.

If I whistled at Otty to summon her she would stop what she was doing and look at me with a mild surmise. If I whistled again with more authority she would smile gently to herself, tongue lolling out, then lope away before human behaviour became even more eccentric.

And it was hopeless to give chase. Otty could accelerate from rest to thirty mph in five yards and maintain that cruising speed indefinitely. She could go even faster out of doors.

I decided on a policy of stealth; Softly, Softly Wettee Otty. Squeezy tube of dog shampoo in left hand, water-bomb in right (as every schoolboy knows, along with 'who imprisoned Montezuma', a water-bomb is a large plastic bag full of water, which explodes on impact, deluging the victim).

This plan was not wholly successful. In retrospect I think that I was wrong to wear gumboots. These not only slow down the bomber's speed to well below thirty knots but the top of the gumboot acts as a funnel which receives the water when the lolloping action of running causes the plastic bag to rupture.

I changed out of gumboots, put on a dry right sock, and resolved that even though I had, at first, not succeeded I would try again. This time with the garden hose.

I shoved the nozzle of the hose down my shirt and strolled nonchalantly towards Otty, who was lying on the grass trying to hypnotise a sparrow into coming within paw range. She eyed me warily. I walked on right past her and waggled my hips, a sign to my wife in the garage to turn the water on. I removed the nozzle from my shirt and waited for the water to come through so that I could swing suddenly round and, to Otty's astonishment, drench her.

No water came. Not a trickle. I waggled my hips furiously. The hose remained dry. I turned to see what had gone wrong and there was Otty, tongue lolling happily, sitting on the hose.

"Off it!" I shouted. "Giddup! Nice Otty! Here girl! Up!" She made no move.

It was then that I made my mistake. In order to have both hands free to wave at Otty I shoved the nozzle of the hose down my trousers. At which moment Otty got off the hose.

How often can the human spirit try again before despair sets in? As I changed into dry trousers I was on the point of giving up when my eye alighted on a newspaper which had been pressed into service to line a drawer. Facing me was a photograph of a riot in Japan. And pictured there was my answer to the problem of how to give Otty a bath; a water-cannon. A device which could saturate a thousand aggrieved Japanese would surely be capable of dampening Otty.

The ironmongers in Egham did not stock water-cannons, I found, but I was able to borrow from Mrs Caddy a device which worked on exactly the same principle. Mrs Caddy called it a Grain Lifter and she used it on her farm to shift grain from a cart up to the top of her silo. It was a vast machine which plugged into the mains and consisted basically of a pipe which was thrust into the grain which needed to be lifted, an electric blower, and another pipe on top which squirted the grain, under great pressure, in whichever direction she wished it to be squirted.

I planned the operation most carefully. The Grain Lifter was towed in by tractor and parked on the lawn. I plugged it in to a 13 amp. plug in the house. The feed tube was inserted into a barrel of rainwater and the gun end was trained upon a spot, some twenty yards away, where I had assembled a little pile of goodies; old raincoats, telephone directories, chamois leathers, peppermints, elderly eggs, string from the Sunday joint – all Otty's favourite foods. We let Otty out of the house and she made immediately for the pile, reassured herself that there was nobody lurking within harmful range, and lay down contentedly for a good chew. I gave the signal to switch the current on.

What happened next can only be described as a blinding flash. The Grain Lifter burst into flames, the main fuses in the house blew, and the neon signs went dim outside every betting-shop within a ten mile radius of Thorpe, Surrey.

The magistrates' court at Guildford took the view that I was entirely to blame. They went on and on about negligence and I must have known that the machine was not designed to be used with water and that the manufacturers had warned users that the machine would not work when dampness was present, and had I not seen the warning printed on the side of the machine?

I had seen the warning but, without my reading glasses, I had taken it for a motto encouraging perseverance. What was actually written across the thing, in humiliatingly large letters, was:

'IF AT FIRST YOU DON'T SUCK SEED, TRY DRIER GRAIN.'

Wonders will never cease

Sir Henry Bate Dudley
(*Letter to Garrick*, 1776)

AS I grow older – a practice I seem to be falling into more frequently these days – I find myself making increasing use of the expression 'mark my words'. Never was the utterance more bandied than in the argument about installing central heating.

I was against it, and eloquently. "When did our island people begin to decline as a world power?" I asked. "When they started living in warm rooms. Take the Victorians, whose homes were bone-achingly cold. Why was it they all went out and conquered tropical countries? Simply to have somewhere they could take their overcoats off. Mark my words, when we lost our goose-pimples, we lost our greatness. Moreover" – that's another word I've taken to, since the prematurely-greys – "moreover, when central heating came in, do you realise what went out? Chilblains! One of the greatest losses the hedonists of this country have ever suffered. Make what claims you will about your wife-swapping and your hard-core and your orgies, the permissive society has come up with no pleasure so purely ecstatic as scratching a chilblain."

I was, as usual, in a minority of one. Despite all my ingenious rear-guard manoeuvres against installation – very strong peppermints, thermal underwear, letting the baby sleep in the airing-cupboard – I was eventually forced to yield to domestic pressures. What finally turned the tide against me was when the District Nurse halted at the bird-cage one December day. "Oh," she exclaimed, "what pretty bluebirds!" On learning they were canaries, she immediately finked to the Health Department.

So it was we began the whole dreary business of Heating Engineers and boilers and radiators and British Thermal Units and "you'll have to run the down-pipe through the master bedroom''. One of the disadvantages of installing central heating in an aging house is that there is no way of hiding the piping. In consequence, every one of our living areas now gives the appearance of a ship's engine-room.

Let me point out another consequence of adding artificial warmth to a house that has managed to exist without it since before Crippen was apprehended. Everything warps. There is, apparently, a scientific law that heat makes things expand and cold makes them contract – the reason, I suppose, why days are longer in the summer and shorter in the winter. And when it comes to heating houses, this scientific law manifests itself by causing every bit of woodwork to swell, twist, curve and curl.

Doors, for example, jam in the half-open position. That is a peculiarly irritating phenomenon for me because I am a man given to dramatic gestures. In any argument, I have made an extremely satisfying practice of storming out of the room and slamming the door behind me. Now you try doing that with a door that jams in the half-open position. Your arm pulls halfway out of its socket.

Equally irritating, but more financially depressing, is what happens to windows. We have wooden sash-windows and when the central heating was put in, during the summer months, they were all open, in the 'up' position. Around November the wind started making BBC Sound Effects noises so I went round the house pulling down their lower halves. What did I come back with? Fourteen snapped sash-cords. The central heating's trial-run had corrugated every window-frame's edge, wedging each one fast within its groove.

"Not to worry," said the carpenter when he called to inspect them. "All it means is supplying and fitting fourteen new window-sections." Then he quoted me a price which could have kept a family of five in the Bahamas for three fun-packed months. "Not on your freelance-writing nelly," said the Bank Manager I went to for the money.

For the rest of the November-to-April period, our rooms, with every window jammed in the open position, presented some fascinatingly varied extremes of temperature. From the new radiators to the middle of the carpet we could have posed for one of those High Speed Gas commercials – everybody smilingly half-dressed and the baby tottering about naked. From the middle of the carpet to the window – Antarctica. On the radiator side of the room, daffodils bloomed. On the window side, edelweiss. The RSPCA said we had the only tortoise with schizophrenia.

I am not an obstinate man. I readily admit that a house without central heating does present certain snags. On a winter's morning it's not always convenient having to run four times round your bedroom before your fingers thaw enough to undo your pyjama buttons. But such a house does possess one important factor in its favour. Mark my words –

"Windows will never seize."

O for the touch of a vanish'd hand

Alfred, Lord Tennyson
'Break, Break, Break'

Fraud

IT was frightful, standing there in the witness box of the North London Magistrate's Court, looking across at my dear old friend and comrade Denis Norden slumped in the dock.

He seemed drawn, as if by Felix Topolski; and his face looked – as indeed the whole of him had been – pinched. It was only a minor charge on which he stood arraigned, thanks be to merciful Providence; a matter of being caught whistling outside the Golders Green Scottish Presbyterian Church on a Sunday afternoon.

The magistrate was talking to me. "This sort of hooliganism has got to be stamped out. It's devil's work, d'ye ken?" he said. "But I'm prepared to give the laddie another wee chance. If I bind him over, will you stand surety for his good behaviour? To the tune of five pounds?"

I leapt at the chance of being the instrument of my colleague's freedom.

"Oh yes, sir!" I exclaimed. "Yes, yes! With all my heart! Indeed I will! Oh, yes and yes again!"

"Have you five pounds?"

"And to spare, sir!" I cried.

"Have you five pounds when all your debts are paid?"

A routine little question they always have to ask. Wasting the court's time. It's a wonder they don't do away with it.

"Yes, sir," I answered stoutly. "And I gladly pledge every. . . ."

I paused. I suddenly felt uneasy. Car not a debt – could be whipped back if instalments not paid. Owed Jim Knight the fishmonger for a pair of kippers – but he owed us for a dozen of our eggs so that was a credit rather than a debit. Why this unease?

76

The mists of memory cleared suddenly. All my debts were most certainly not paid. I had one outstanding debt, years old, and I had no idea how large the amount was.

It must have been about eleven years ago when the debt was incurred. At that time my wife and I had a canal boat, 'SAMANDA', in which we used to potter up and down the Inland Waterways when the summer wasn't too rigorous. I suppose that in a good year we spent about ten days actually afloat in her but we were privileged, as proud owners, to spend every spare hour from September to May scrubbing, derusting, painting and varnishing her so that she wouldn't disintegrate one day when we weren't looking; a trick that boats have.

That summer the drizzle was particularly warm so we decided to take 'SAMANDA' up the Oxford canal and round into the Grand Union, taking in the Blisworth tunnel, which is over a mile and a half long.

Halcyon days they were, with halcyons swooping over the water in a flash of glittering blue.

Occasionally we towed the boat along from the towpath in blissful silence, but we usually used the motor because the tow-rope chafed my wife's neck.

It was all so magical until we got halfway through Blisworth tunnel. Now canal tunnels are pitch dark, moist, and there is just room for two boats to pass. Just.

Half-way through the Blisworth we heard the sound that every Inland Waterway mariner dreads, the thump-thump-thump of an approaching narrow-boat's diesel engine. Narrow-boats are the old canal working boats, over seventy feet in length, made of steel, or elm planks about a foot thick, and one touch from them can stove in the hull of a fancy little cruiser like ours.

We switched off our engine and clung to the wall on our side of the tunnel, slightly alarmed by a regular series of dull thuds which got louder as the narrow-boat got nearer. When she came into our head-light beam the reason for the thuds became apparent. The narrow-boat was chugging up the tunnel towards us ricocheting from one wall to the other, clearly unmanned.

"It's the 'Flying Dutchman'!" I yelled.

"What, up the Grand Union canal?" replied my wife. "With nobody on board? No, be sensible. If anything it's the 'Marie Celeste'."

In fact it was the 'Alfred J. Crump'. We found out later that it had been hired by a couple of middle-aged ladies who didn't fancy going

77

through the tunnel so left the engine in gear and hurried over the top to catch the boat at the other end.

By some miracle we were not sunk. The narrow-boat passed by in mid-bounce, but there was a board sticking out of its side which caught our craft a glancing blow at the bows.

"Thank Heavens!" my wife cried. "The only damage is a scratch on the 'AND' of 'SAMANDA'."

"But it's a deep scratch!" I said. "In my lovely varnishwork!"

As soon as we had moored up at the next village I went round asking where I could find a painter who would touch up our boat for us.

I should have known something was wrong when the painter arrived, a most distinguished-looking gentleman with a box of paints, an easel, and an umbrella. He seemed a little surprised when I explained what was wanted but he did a splendid job. It took him about two hours. He used best artist's quality varnish because I sneaked a look at the tin.

When he had finished I pumped his hand enthusiastically and congratulated him on his skill, commanding him to send his bill on to me. We exchanged names.

It was only later, when we were on the homeward leg of our journey, that I glanced at the card he had given me and found that the obliging painter who had touched up our name plate was the President of the Royal Academy.

And his bill has yet to arrive. The mind boggles as to how much two hours of the President of the Royal Academy's time costs. Hundreds? Thousands?

My reverie was broken by the magistrate.

"I asked you whether you have five pounds when your debts are paid!"

"I don't know, sir!" I blurted. "You see, sir, I've just remembered. I have one bill outstanding. So you'd better clap my friend in the clink, sir. You see, sir, I'm afraid I still . . . it's not my fault because he hasn't sent it, but I still . . ."

"You still what, man?"

"Owe for the touch of a varnished 'AND'."

Charity begins at home

Sir Thomas Browne
'*Religio Medici*'

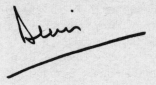

"A MONG the contributors," read the third paragraph of the letter from the publishing firm, "will be Alexander Solzhenitsyn, Dr Christian Barnard, Lord Hailsham, Mother Teresa and other Television Personalities. The book's title will be *My Most Embarrassing Moment* and we would like its opening chapter to be contributed by you."

When I put the letter down, I could not disguise my pleasure. In addition to the natural gratification I felt at being included among such distinguished company, there was also the knowledge they had picked the right man for the right job. For if my life has been rich in no other ways, where moments of embarrassment are concerned shake hands with a millionaire. The trouble, if anything, was going to be that I had too many to choose from, an embarrassment of embarrassments.

I allowed my mind to wander over some of the more neck-reddening of the incidents. The occasion when a large dog followed me into a telephone box and I couldn't get the door open again? The backstage party given by The London Symphony Orchestra when I decided to slip away unobtrusively and walked right through a harp? The day I took a full-size cactus plant on a crowded Underground train? That moment during the Old Fashioned Waltz with the Lady Mayoress at the Huddersfield Press Ball when I realised that my left-hand contact lens had dropped into her cleavage? The time I spilled a whole cup of hot Bovril into my lap – at a nudist camp?

The mere remembrance of these and similar episodes gave me shudders sufficient to keep my automatic wrist-watch running for three days. However, were any of them, in these particular circumstances, really embarrassing *enough*? For an incident to deserve its place as the opening chapter of that book, surely it must identify itself immediately as an absolute nadir of experience, a true North Finchley of the soul.

Well, as with moments of sex, so with moments of embarrassment: it is often the most recent one that is remembered as the most significant. And as, at that time, my most recent one had happened no more than a month ago – moment of embarrassment, I mean – that was the one I decided to record and submit.

The story started with the fact that, when one of the new take-away shops on the Parade went out of business – there just isn't the demand for organic beefburgers round here – a Japanese gentleman took over the premises and opened it as a Karate Academy. In no time at all he was raking in over a hundred quid a week teaching the neighbouring bourgeoisie how to break planks with their bare hands; to say nothing of the extra tenner or so he knocked up doing a sideline in firewood.

Why was I among the first to enrol? Many reasons, the main one being that having grown up on a cultural diet of those magazines with I Was a Seven Stone Weakling on the inside back cover, I hated acknowledging that, even today, if a bully were to kick sand in my girl's face on the beach I'd probably end up helping him.

The strange thing was, something within me responded to Karate. I was a natural. Within four weeks, Mr Sen informed me that I was probably the best fighting pupil he had, better even than old Mrs Willett. Straightaway I made a silent vow that I would never use my powers for evil, only for good.

I'm going to go into the Historic Present tense now, because it's necessary that the next sequence of events be related as graphically as possible. That night, I'm coming home from the Academy and what do I see? Under a lamp post, two people are struggling. One is a well-built young man, the other a rather frail girl, and he's trying to wrest a handbag from her hands. She is kicking at his shins and struggling, but he's so much bigger than she is there can only be one outcome.

So – Karate-time, folks. In two rapid strides I step between them, raise my right arm and, with the heel of the hand – Hah! Ah! Ha-so! Three beautifully timed strikes, like a cobra, and there he lies – writhing on the ground! The girl gazes at me for a moment, then she seizes my hand and presses it to her soft cheek. Releasing it, she snatches up the handbag and runs off into the night.

Chest swelling, I give the big fellow a nudge with my toe. "On your feet, chummy," I say. "We're going down the nick." He stirs and looks up at me. I notice he has a strangely melting gaze. "Too jolly right we jolly are," he says.

"What do you mean?"

"That was *my* handbag."

Although *My Most Embarrassing Moment* has proved to be a voluminous tome, running to some eight hundred-odd pages, the Editorial Board have unanimously agreed that my contribution fully deserves its position as the opening chapter – a fact which their advertising boys were not slow to pick up. Indeed, it has become the sub-head on most of the publicity releases:

'Karate Begins A Tome.'

What's the good of a home if you are never in it?

George and Weedon Grossmith
'The Diary of a Nobody'

Frank

THE other morning at breakfast time I was sitting over a cup of hot coffee when I had a terrific idea. I wasn't even trying to think at the time; I was crouched over the cup trying to steam an egg stain out of the seat of my jeans. If I had a thought in my head at the time it was never again to put a tray with a soft-boiled egg on my chair, move forwards to switch on the television, then back gently and sit down on the egg. If I had been in a thinking mood I might have reflected further on the extraordinary amount of egg there is in an egg; enough in one small oval shell to besmear a cheek and a half of jeans.

But my mind was blank, and into it floated this idea. If pressed for a comparison in the world of nature I would say that it was not at all unlike a mushroom spoor alighting on a damp flannel.

Now every writer dreams about inventing a new character to write novels about. Think how excited Ian Fleming must have been when he dreamed up James Bond, or Galsworthy when he thought of Forsyte Saga. Once a writer has his hero, his Bond or his Saga, the rest is easy; best-sellers, major motion-pictures, television serials.

My idea was a totally original character – a criminal pixie. Or, to put it another way, a bent elf.

For the next three days I put everything else aside and worked like a madman on the plot of the book; I refused all offers of food – except at meal-times, of course – and went without sleep all day, but at the end of it I had a synopsis roughed out.

There are four of them in the gang. Our hero, Norm the Gnome, is the leader. He is a criminal but we make it clear that he is not all that nasty. Nasty-ish but not revolting. He learned his bad habits when he did his National Service – two years in the National Elf Service – and has never since come to terms with society.

Norm's girl-friend is Mustard-Seed, hot stuff, still a bit green, although well past her salad-days. She earns her living as a dancer in the clubs, where she works under her professional name of 'Caustic-Soda'. She is a stripper.

The heavy is Alf the Elf, a huge muscle-bound giant – a giant, that is, up against the elves – who gets all the dirty work to do. He is well known to the police because he unthinkingly allowed himself to be photographed in the nude, rippling his muscles, for the cover of the magazine *Elf and Strength*.

The last member of the group is Puck (real name Robin Badfellow), a layabout who spends most of his time filing his nails and passing remarks. His job with the gang is to act as contact-man and drive the getaway car when they can afford to buy one.

The gang always met on Tuesday evenings because it was a bad night on the telly and one Tuesday Norm strode in very purposefully with a Master Plan.

"Right," he said. "From tonight this gang stops being cat burglars. We've had a good year burgling cats but the market for hot cat-collars even with a bell attached, is satiated. We're going into the big time."

Consternation, as you might well imagine, reigned. The pros and cons were discussed with some heat, but Norm was adamant.

"I'm going to be Mr Big," he said. "Caesar of the Undergrowth. Drive round in an Elfa-Romeo. Take Mustard-Seed to the South of France, first-class on the Cross-Channel Fairy. So here's what we're gonna do. Next Saturday evening, after the Western on telly, we're going to rob a bank!"

"I know a bank whereon the wild thyme blows," said Puck, combing his hair with a thistle.

"That's the one we're going to do!" said Norm.

"I can't manage Saturday," said Puck. "I'll be in the middle of an ice-hockey match."

"Then Mustard-Seed can be look-out," said Norm. "We're going to nick all the thyme from that bank and then take it to a fence."

"Which fence?"

"The one at the bottom of my garden. We'll pin it out on the fence to dry, then put it into packets marked 'Dried Herbs' and flog it to Health Food addicts up the Goblin Market. There's a fortune in it."

"Hey boss," said Alf the Elf, to everybody's surprise as he didn't go in much for talking. "We'll get caught. That bank's floodlit!"

Norm silenced him with a look. "We are going to tunnel!" he announced. "I have recruited Mo the Mole and Harry Hedgehog for the job. We are going to go in underneath the plants and pull them up – *downwards!*"

Everything seemed to be going according to plan on the night. Mo the Mole burrowed a rough tunnel, then Harry the Hedgehog went in and scraped the tunnel smooth with his quills. The roots of the thyme dangled down. Norm dragged the thyme down by its roots and passed it to Alf, who staggered down the tunnel and deposited it in piles outside. And then something went wrong. Alf had disappeared with the last load when Norm had a gnomish feeling that all was not well. He ran down the tunnel to the entrance – and it was blocked. He was trapped by a large clod of turf, which had been rolled over the entrance.

"Somebody has grassed on me!" he groaned. And sat down to wait for the police.

The story ends with Norm the Gnome staring through his prison bars, while Mustard-Seed dances cheek to cheek with Puck in some thieves' hangout, humming to herself, "Thyme on my hands, you in my arms. . . ."

I really thought I had a winner in Norm, the delinquent Gnome. Original, dramatic, suitable for all age-groups. But I was wrong. He is useless to me, as I found out when I telephoned a publisher.

I telephoned the best publisher in London. I cannot, of course, mention his name but he was out so I spoke to his wife, Mrs Eyre Methuen.

"I've thought of this wonderful character for a book," I said. "He's a bent gnome called . . ."

That was as far as I got.

"A gnome?" she cried. "A *gnome?* You can't write books about a gnome! That's Enid Blyton's territory. You might be able to get away with writing about a gnome if you were another Enid Blyton, but that is what you will never be."

And so it has all been for nothing. I still have my beautiful little character, the crooked Norm, but I have to face facts:

"What's the good of a gnome if you're never Enid?"

Give your thoughts no tongue,
Nor any unproportion'd thought his act

William Shakespeare
'Hamlet'

[signature]

ONE of the many profound experiences which people without children are deprived of is that of sitting through a small daughter's Dancing Class Concert. I was conscripted for this numbness one long-ago Christmas when my daughter was six years old.

The reason she had joined the class in the first place was because she had somehow got herself mixed-up with a boy there. By mixed-up, I'm not implying she was mistaken for him, I mean there was an emotional involvement. It was a relationship I frowned upon, not merely because the lad bore a striking facial resemblance to Joan Crawford – after all, so does Mick Jagger – but because he was going on for at least twelve and I never believe there's any future in those May and December things. Also, and perhaps unreasonably, I had a sneaking feeling that any boy who voluntarily joins a Dancing Class cannot be all good.

However even at six, my daughter had, as they say, a whim of iron, so I took her along to meet the Principal. That lady's name was Signora Estrellita Mariposa which I didn't believe for a second, especially as her husband's name was Ornstein. She took against my child on sight. The moment we entered the room, "Much too tall!" was her opening comment. I immediately bristled, thinking she was referring to me, but la Signora went on to aver that, for a member of a juvenile dancing troupe, the ideal specification is 'winsomely tiny'. Now while it is true that we are a lanky family and my daughter could have signed for the Harlem Globetrotters almost at birth, such a summary dismissal offended all my principles of equality in the arts. I therefore argued the case powerfully, and after a certain amount of wallet-waving Signora Mariposa consented to allow her assistant to take the child into the next room for an audition.

"This one is a natural mover," announced that lady on their return, rather giving the impression that some six-year-olds had been found to be battery operated. With bad grace and at an exorbitant fee, the Principal agreed to take the child aboard.

The ensuing months I remember mainly for the nightly thumps on the ceiling as practice took place upstairs but the high point was reached in mid-November. "I'm going to be a Snowball!" exulted my daughter when she returned from class one cold evening. Some narrow-eyed questioning elicited the explanation that in the forth-coming annual concert – 'Santa Claus's Workshop!, A Seasonal Extravaganza Of Song and Dance' – my daughter had won the coveted role over stiff opposition. "It's ninepence a ticket and every-body's got to come along and clap me," she ordered.

Everybody turned out to be me, all other blood-relations having had the foresight to develop Asian flu or go wintering in the Canary Isles. So, on that bleak December afternoon, I made my way to the concert's venue, the Cinema Café of the local Odeon.

All Cinema Cafés have a doomed air at the best of times, but on this occasion it was sheer Camus. And while we're on the literary references, you know that line of Sartre's about 'Hell is other people'? Well, it isn't. It's other people's *children*. There were sixty-seven pupils in that Dancing Class and every single one had a featured part in the two-and-a-half hour production. An unending parade of tidy winsomes, all of them bedaubed in lip-stick and greasepaint and red dots in the corners of their eyes, like a procession of depraved midgets.

I did notice, though, that the entrance of each one was greeted by loud localised plaudits from whichever area of the auditorium his or her family group was located. This showed me where my own duty lay. "When my child comes on," I vowed, "I will make up in vocifer-ousness what I lack in numbers."

So when the orchestra – Miss Larby on piano and tambourine – struck up 'Winter Wonderland', I was ready. From the months of overhead thumping I knew this to be the tune to which we did our bit, so I took a deep breath. And when that glittering white Snowball tittuped on from behind the papier-mâché icicles, I rose to my feet and let out the full Sammy Davis Jnr whoop. "Wah-hoo! Yowee! Great, great! The kid's a sensation! Let's hear it for a really wonderful performer! Encore, encore! A-one more time!"

It was when the Snowball burst into terrified tears that I realised two elements were amiss. One, her physique was of an unfamiliar tinyness; two, there were twenty-three other Snowballs entering behind her.

I had, as was explained to me afterwards, whooped it up for the wrong Snowball. My daughter was number sixteen in the Snowball line. At the time though, the father of the hysterical Snowball spun round and punched me in the throat. I kicked him in the elbow (no, I can't think how), the police were called, I was ejected and Signora Mariposa summarily withdrew my daughter from the Concert, not even allowing her to stay and wave in the Finale. "I shall never permit a tall tot on stage again," she snarled.

Next day she expelled her from the class completely, claiming that the whole ugly incident would never have taken place had it not been for the child's excessive height. My daughter, for her part, blamed the whole thing on me and left home as soon as she reached adolescence. She is now in North Cornwall living with an unemployed rifle-range attendant who bears a striking facial resemblance to Linda Darnell.

I can only hope that the sorry tale offers a guide-line to any other fathers who may have small daughters about to appear in Dancing Class Concerts. Unless they are of the requisite tinyness – keep your mouth shut when they make their entrance. As Polonius advised Laertes:

"Give your tots no tongue,
For any unproportion'd tot is sacked."

Half a loaf is better than no bread

Proverb

Frank

OH, believe me, it is not all glamour and laughter being Bimbo the Clown. Lots of you must have seen me when Potter and Ginsberg's Mammoth Imperial Circus visited your town. We usually pitched our big top in the car-park behind the pub.

I was the comic little chappie with baggy trousers and a ginger wig who ran on after the elephant. It was, from time to time, dangerous work.

Now no man is made of wood, not even Woden, The Wooden Man – he had a wooden leg but the rest of him was painted and grained to match it – and there came a time when I felt the urge to marry and settle down.

But who would marry Bimbo the Clown? What lady would be happy to say "That's my husband over there", pointing to a tiny, white-faced figure in enormous boots, with a red ping-pong ball nose, sitting in a bucket of whitewash? During most of my appearances I was deluged with whitewash. I had so much of it poured over me that my first thought when we arrived at a new town was to find a vet and get my distemper inoculation.

The first lady I approached with a view to courtship was Rumpo, the Fat Lady. Like many vast ladies she was a gentle, kindly person, always willing to help out when a lorry got stuck in the mud. One day the electricity in my caravan went off when I was in the middle of doing my ironing and Rumpo went down on all fours and turned the generator by hand. So I pressed my suit on her.

When I took her to Brighton on our day off everything seemed set fair. I had a little Mini at that time so I hired a van and away we went, as happy as two children let out of school. We even found a children's playground and played seesaw, Rumpo on one end and me and the van on the other. But tragedy struck later that night on the way home. I had stopped the van and helped Rumpo out of the back to give the springs a rest. As my arm went round part of her waist I suddenly blurted out my secret wish that I might one day make her Mrs Bimbo.

She burst into laughter. She howled with mirth that I could ever think she would marry a clown. As I worked the handle and jacked her up into the back of the van my heart was near breaking point.

Hath not a clown eyes? Hath not a clown hands, affections, passions? If you prick us, do not jets of water squirt out from our eyebrows? If you tickle us, doth not our ginger wig stand on end and the toes of our boots emit steam? If you poison us, doth not our bow-tie revolve?

Hurt and bruised, I scarcely spoke to another lady for some years. Then the side-show department of the circus acquired a new attraction, George-Ina, Half-Man Half-Woman. From delicate oval face to hairy legs, a vision of delight.

I was immediately attracted. There was a natural reticence there which appealed to me. Many circus-folk are over-friendly and are forever popping into your caravan but George-Ina, well – he kept himself to herself.

Perhaps the affair might have gone no further had not fate stepped in. One Sunday evening I returned late to the big top to hear screams and shouts. And George-Ina's unmistakable voice:

"HE-lp!''

A terrible scene greeted me as I rushed in. It seems that Flexo, the Indiarubber Man, had been on one of his benders. He was clutching George-Ina to him and, inflamed with cheap liquor, was threatening that unless she agreed to spend the night in his caravan he would release the lion from its cage to claw all and sundry.

Everybody from the circus was there, and they all turned to me.

"Flexo," I said levelly. "You're twisted."

He merely snarled.

An icy calm came over me. Putting on my ping-pong nose to give myself confidence I moved unobtrusively to the side of Madam Zaza, the Human Cannonball, and said to her, very quietly:

"Madam Zaza, will you do me the pleasure of inserting yourself up your cannon, fusing yourself where necessary?"

She slipped away like a shadow.

Affecting nonchalance, I sauntered towards the cannon, muttering to the others as I passed, "Hide behind something in case Madam Zaza ricochets."

Once at the cannon I swiftly swung it until the muzzle pointed straight at the Indiarubber Man's heart.

"All right, Flexo!" I shouted, a new authority in my voice. "Drop George-Ina and walk slowly forwards with your hands above your head. Make one false move and I'll fill you full of Madam Zaza!"

He knew he was beaten. He unhanded George-Ina and stumbled forward. At that moment the local police arrived and took him away. The Indiarubber Man is now in Wormwood Scrubs prison, doing a stretch.

George-Ina fell into my waiting arms, and suddenly we were alone under the big top.

"Dear sir/madam," I whispered, "will you be mine?"

"I wish I could make up my mind." George-Ina whispered back. "Half of me wants to, but the other half is not so sure. . . ."

"Then let me make your mind up for you!" I cried, and picking her up in my arms I ran with her to the sideshow marked See the Vicar Starving In A Barrel, where the vicar kindly interrupted his supper long enough to marry us.

People sometimes ask me whether I have not missed something, sharing my life with somebody who is half a gentleman and half a lady. Perhaps. But on a wintry evening, when we are snug in our caravan, me washing the whitewash out of my smalls, George-Ina varnishing her nails or lighting up her pipe, I think to myself – why cry for the moon when I have the stars?

Half a love is better than no bride.

THE most eloquent example of graffiti I can recall seeing was written on a road-sign. Under the notice 'Cul de Sac' someone had scrawled the words 'What isn't?'

Even if I had failed to recognise the handwriting, the sentiment would have identified the writer for me: Neville Pacefoot, the text-book example of what pop psychiatrists call 'a victim personality'. From early childhood, life treated him like the back wall of a squash court.

Neville's first brush with calamity came during his Boy Scout days. While he was helping an old lady across a street they both got run over. After a three-hour operation, he was taken off the danger-list and they allowed him to sit up and look at his Get Well cards. The first one was so amusing, he burst out laughing and broke eight stitches. Opening the next one he cut his finger and developed blood-poisoning.

Those were the earliest intimations that, in this supermarket we call Existence, Neville had grabbed the shopping-cart with the wonky wheel. At the outbreak of War he persuaded the RAF to accept him, despite the fact that two of his toes had been crushed shapeless. (By a falling First Aid Cabinet.) He immediately became the only serviceman to get wounded during his Preliminary Medical Examination. While the Medical Officer was sounding his chest, Neville noticed an Air Vice-Marshal entering the room, so he threw up a salute. It pulled the rubber tube of the stethoscope clean out of the M.O.'s head, and when the metal ear-pieces snapped back, that was the last of Neville's teeth. Nevertheless he persevered with the training and passed out as Sergeant Air Gunner.

The stripes did not survive his first mission. He spent that whole trip to and from Hamburg with his face pressed against the fuselage, the result of having slammed his handle-bar moustache in the plane door just before take-off. Invalided out with a disability pension a few months later, having been run over by an ambulance, he was directed to agricultural work and spent six months on a farm before a cow fell on him.

I lost touch with Neville for a while after the War, although I kept reading about him in such periodicals as the *Journal Of The Road Accident Research Centre*, whose cover he made four times. After he'd achieved national headlines as the first driver to break a leg by catching his foot in a car safety-belt, his insurance company wrote to ask for their calendar back. "It's like giving life cover to a lemming," the letter said.

It was round about this time that Neville's wife finally decided to leave him. For some time now she had found herself writing lipstick messages like "Enough's enough!" across the bedroom mirror, but when it was discovered that their daughter had been put in the family way by their son's Probation Officer, Mrs Pacefoot called it a day. She was given custody of the house, the furniture and the children, leaving Neville with only his savings, which had been safely invested in a pharmaceutical company making cyclamates.

From then on, things went steadily downhill. Fired from his job – his employer claimed that Neville's frequent trips to Intensive Care Units were inconsistent with being Manager of a Health Food Shop – he was obliged to seek whatever work he could. The day he was caught in the rain while carrying two thousand free samples of a new detergent, Neville gave way to despair and 'phoned the Samaritan organisation. The line was engaged.

How deeply his self-confidence had been shaken I did not realise till our next meeting. It took place as usual in a Casualty Ward, this time at St Mary's, where he had been rushed after swallowing a fishbone.

"Well, that's not unique," I said consolingly. "That happens to lots of people."

"Not when they're eating a chocolate mousse."

I discounted the strain in his tone at first, putting it down to the fact that he was also awaiting trial on a serious charge. While driving along the Bayswater Road, he'd put his hand out to indicate a right turn. His signal coincided with the arrival alongside of a motor-cycle policeman who had accelerated up to Neville's window to congratulate him on his courteous driving. Neville's hand smashed him right in the mouth.

"You must try and look on the bright side," I said. "Worse things happen at sea."

"I've been at sea," he said. "I was the only person on board to get lockjaw and seasickness at the same time. Know what I'm beginning to think? I'm coming round to the conclusion that perhaps life isn't a cabaret, old chum."

I must admit to some feeling of uneasiness when I bade him farewell and, in the event, my forebodings were justified. Neville left the hospital with every intention of making his quittance of life. The notion of throwing himself in front of a train seemed a fitting response to a world which had placed so many hazards in his own path.

He made his way swiftly to King's Cross but just outside the station he was halted by someone tugging his sleeve. It was an old woman. "Spare a silver piece, kind sir," she said. "Only a small silver piece."

"What for? he asked.

"A sprig of lucky white heather."

Despite the fact that fate had blunted most of Neville's physical features, his sense of irony remained keen. With a faint smile he handed her his last pound-note and thrust the sprig of heather into his button-hole. There was something to be relished in the idea of casting himself in the path of a fast express while wearing a good-luck token.

Making his way to the platform where the 3.35 to Carlisle stood, he stationed himself in front of the engine. When the guard blew his whistle, he closed his eyes tightly, waited to hear the first turn of the mighty wheels, then flung himself forward.

Philosophical profundities are not really my speed but I will venture to offer you a small one: when you're a loser – it's no use even expecting to win. The train went out backwards.

A lady porter picked Neville up off the line and dusted him down. As she was due to go off duty in a few minutes anyway, she took him home with her and gave him a cup of tea, with some of her home-made ginger cake.

He's now living with her in quite blissful sin just outside Leatherhead, where they're running a small but thriving everything-shop.

Its name? Well, I suppose, in a wry kind of way, it's appropriate: THE WHITE HEATHER STORES.

93

'Goodbye, Mr Chips'

James Hilton
Title of Novel

Frank

I am usually such a happy little chap, ever ready to dispel gloom with a merry quip or a saucy *bon mot*. I don't think that I would be breaking a confidence if I reveal that many years ago the lady with a mole who taught Sunday School at the Congregational Church referred to me as 'one of Nature's sunbeams'.

But a few months ago, I changed. Instead of dashing about the house wreathed in smiles and throwing off jolly epigrams I took to leaning silently against the wallpaper, scowling and plucking at the hem of my jacket.

The change came over me one day when I was lunching at the BBC canteen. I looked down at my tray, veal-loaf fritters and a waffle, and the awful realisation dawned that the meal epitomised my career; frittering my time away, and waffling on the radio. I had achieved nothing for which I would be remembered by posterity.

But what to do about it? What mark does one have to make so that when one is dead and gone one will be remembered long after one is forgotten?

The answer came to me on a bench in Hyde Park, where I was sitting brooding. A Japanese tourist beside me was fanning his face with a folded copy of the *Evening Standard* and a headline caught my eye; 'Paul Getty pays £15,000 for National Gallery's "Washerwoman". This seemed to me to be a stiff price to pay for recruiting domestic staff, even for a man reputedly not short of a bob, so my curiosity was aroused. I found that by getting on my knees in front of the man and synchronising my head with the oscillations of the newspaper I could read the whole piece. What emerged from the article was that Paul Getty had bought a terra-cotta portrait head from the National

Gallery. It was a study by Rodin of his washerwoman, Mme Gautier. She was a friendly, excitable woman, aged thirty-four, with two daughters, etc. etc.

Of course! The way to go down to posterity is to be sculptured! If the biography of an unknown washerwoman could, a hundred years after her death, still cool the brow of a Japanese tourist, surely the same fame would attend me? I can see the newspaper article now – 'A terra-cotta head changed hands for £15,000,000 today. It is reputedly the head of F. Muir, who lived a hundred years ago. Now famous, he was little known at the time being by trade a fritterer and waffler. A lady with a mole once called him "one of Nature's sunbeams", and certainly his noble brow betokens . . .' etc.

I set to at once to sculpt a terra-cotta head of myself to present to the National Gallery.

It seemed to me that the best way to ensure a likeness would be to work from photographs. So I persuaded the Egham Photographic Society to help. Eighty of them turned up one sunny Saturday. I formed them into a circle, stood in the middle, 'click', and a week later I had eighty photographs of my head, each taken from a slightly different angle.

The next problem was the terra-cotta. I always thought the word referred to beefy nursemaids who hurled the baby into its cot, but it turned out to be reddish clay. Happily our house is on gravel soil so I only had to dig down some five feet before striking clay. It was somewhat yellow so I mixed it with a tin of dark-brown boot-polish.

I had about enough terra-cotta to make two heads, each about the size of a grapefruit, so I decided to make a test run on one of the lumps first, just in case sculpting was more difficult than it looked.

I bashed the clay into shape with my fists and then pushed it about with a spoon and a toothpick until it began to look something like a human head. I was not attempting a likeness this time, which was a good thing because I had managed to get both ears on the same side. And three nostrils to the one nose.

Then into the oven it went, one hour at Regulo Mark 4.

When it came out – disaster. For some reason the whole head had slumped and spread. It still looked vaguely like a head but the head of a baboon.

"It's bound to sag when it's all in a lump," said my wife. "It's the same with pastry. What you want to do is treat it like we do a pie.

Make it hollow, fill it with dried peas so that it keeps its shape, then lay the top on, pinching the edges together as you do with pastry."

Which is what I did. It was a tricky operation with a tacky lump of clay-and-boot-polish, and it took nearly a pound of dried peas to fill it, but I managed it. Then I lined up my eighty photographs, took spoon in hand, and started.

Who can explain the workings of fate? Was it a fluke? Was it the awakening of latent genius? All I can say for sure is that after ten minutes with spoon and toothpick I had produced a startling likeness of myself, an amazing little portrait head which the National or any other gallery would be proud to shove in a glass case next to the postcard counter in the foyer. I shouted for my wife to come and see it.

"Incredible!" she breathed. "So lifelike, and exact. And, sort of, peaceful!"

"So it should be," I replied. "It's full of peas." (I was quite my old self again).

With infinite care we carried the head through to the kitchen and slid it into the cooker. As my wife closed the oven door I drew a chair up to the oven and prepared for a long vigil.

"No you don't!" said my wife. "There's nothing more you can do until the clay is baked. Let's go to the pictures."

It was a Saturday, and on Saturdays my son often dropped in. He had finished at university and was working in the City. Down a hole in the City, digging up Roman remains before office blocks cemented them away for ever. It was his practice to nip home sometime over the weekend with his pockets full of clothes to be washed, stand up in the bath and scrape Thames mud and medieval effluent off his salient features, eat whatever he could find in the house as long as it was hot and preferably smothered in chips, and disappear, leaving a laconic note on the kitchen table.

We arrived home from the pictures. I made straight for the oven. As I had my hand on the oven door I heard my wife saying, "Hello, Jamie's been home. Funny. I don't remember leaving out a –"

At that moment I opened the oven door to look at my masterpiece. And the oven was empty.

I knew instinctively what had happened, of course. "Farewell posterity," I whispered to myself as I held my hand out for Jamie's note.

Yes, there it was in black and white. Just five words:

"Good pie. Missed the chips".